CREATOCRACY

CREATOCRACY

How the Constitution Invented Hollywood

Elizabeth Wurtzel

Thought Catalog Books

Brooklyn, NY

First edition, 2015

ISBN 978-1-57687-770-8

10 9 8 7 6 5 4 3 2 1

Printed and bound in Canada

Founded in 2010, Thought Catalog is a website and imprint
dedicated to your ideas and stories. We publish fiction and
non-fiction from emerging and established writers across all
genres. Learn more at www.thoughtcatalog.com/about.

Cover photography by Jason Myers

for Chris Lavergne, who saw

"Progress is our most important product."

—Ronald Reagan, for General Electric

"In the unlikely story that is America, there is nothing false about hope."

—Barack Obama

1

The American flag is the most exquisite and artistic of all the banners of all the nations. One hangs over my sofa, so I look at the Stars and Stripes quite a lot. The asymmetry of its exotic design cannot be explained by the fad for Greek Revival architecture that is another contemporaneous remnant of 1776. For some wacky reason, Betsy Ross—the mythic seamstress, much like Dolley Madison is the First Lady of ice cream—stuck the blue patch of white stars in the corner, when by all rights it ought to be in the center. Perhaps she simply ran out of thread before she got to sew on some missing piece, perhaps this is a gorgeous mistake the way Post-its are a failed attempt to produce paper squares that would stick permanently. Or perhaps this is more like the case of the Maccabees, their miracle of making one day's supply of olive oil last for eight: They got Hanukah, we got America.

Ever since it has been inadvertent brilliance, this

country has been one big huge accident, slouching toward perfection.

Nowadays, of course, we're so used to the off-kilter geometry of the American flag that we don't even notice it, the way we don't notice that American exceptionalism is completely for real, for better and for worse. But in 1776, the normal thing to do was the normal thing to do. To stick a square in one corner but not the others was odd: In the eighteenth century, nothing was deliberately uneven. Clearly, Mrs. Ross was either out of cloth or out of her mind. More to the point, the Founding Fathers who took on this odd mismatch or mishmash of clashing patterns of striped astronomy must have been very advanced: They were the first modern artists. Ask Jasper Johns. The Founders were far out, very far out, in the truest sense: the denotation that is the connotation.

This country was always cool.

Everything we do here is cooler than everything they do everywhere else, and so it will ever be. We will never necessarily be more compassionate or more intelligent, but we will be more grand and creative. Maybe the Chinese know math better because they count grains of rice or something, but American sixteen-year-olds invent apps on a dime—and America invented the sixteen-year-old. We have sixteen-year-olds galore, more and more all the time. We have stupid sixteen-year-olds inventing stupid apps that everyone in China wants.[1]

And we so take our flag for granted that few of us notice that it is a modern masterpiece.

"I am large, I contain multitudes," wrote Walt Whitman in 1855, the first voice of America in "Song of Myself," which was really the song of all our selves.

The defining characteristic of America is our fanaticism: We dream big, we think large, we create grandeur. We invented Hollywood, rock 'n' roll, blue jeans, the Gold Rush, cable TV with thousands of channels, a military that is larger than those of the next ten combined, the shopping mall, and a store that sells nothing but socks. We invented Elvis Presley and teen idols, we invented the phonograph and the movie camera, we invented Disneyland and the roller coaster, baseball and apple pie. We invented the Internet—oh, yes we did—and the anonymous comment. We didn't invent the wheel, but we did come up with the Model T; we didn't invent the wing, but we did give the world the airplane and the miracle of flight. We didn't invent the computer, but we did invent the PC and everything that everyone can do at home; we didn't invent the telephone, but we did invent the iPhone and everything that everyone can do in the palm of his hand. We invented Thomas Edison and Henry Ford and

1. Matt Richtel, "The Youngest Technorati," *The New York Times* (March 8, 2014). http://www.nytimes.com/2014/03/09/technology/the-youngest-technorati.html?_r=0

Steve Jobs: so there. We invented the world we live in: so *there*.

And we came up with the notion that a single nation can span a third of a continent and contain fifty different states, each with its own character, none of which believes it ought to be its own country. In Europe, even Czecho-slovakia cannot bear to remain a single nation. Africa can barely hold itself together as a continent. Mazel tov on the Arab Spring. But it's boring to list all the places hell-bent on fragmentation. Here, somehow, we are one nation under a groove. We have too much to do and we are extremely busy. We invent things, we invent everything: Since this nation came to be, almost every important invention under creation happened here, because America is the coolest invention of all.

This country is now undeniably, tragically, inexorably in decline, but given all we have and all we have done, we still have centuries to go. Consider this: Nowhere else but here can you get half & half with your coffee. This is not a great technological invention, but rather a simple mix-ture of cream and milk that makes even the unbearable brown stuff that's been burned from sitting in a rusty urn too long okay to drink. And yet, great metropolises like London and Paris and Tel Aviv and Shanghai might maybe have full-fat milk somewhere or other in the kitchen if you ask, which is not the same. If the rest of the world can't come close on a basic dairy product, is there any point to the rest of the world?

What would the world be without America?

It would be a dull and dinky planet, indeed.

2

The American Constitution, one of our first inventions, is also very cool, but more in the sense of Marshall McLuhan's medium cool: It is not a warm document. Structural and skeletal, it is a sparse and spare affair of fewer than three thousand words. As Hannah Arendt pointed out, when the Framers composed the Constitution, "it concerned not the order of society, but the form of government."[1] So it plots a Google Maps route through a tripartite, bicameral, presidential, republican democracy. It allots the powers necessary to govern, and little more; it metes out what is needed and leaves the rest to the people and the states. The Constitution concerns itself with collecting taxes, coining money, raising an army, electing leaders, organizing courts, enforcing contracts, naturalizing citizens, regulating trade—the stuff of running a country. There are no flowery entitlements, no fanciful

---

1. Hannah Arendt, *On Revolution* (Penguin Classics, 1990), 68.

flourishes, no pretty promises—even the Bill of Rights, the more famous addendum, is not about what the government can do for us so much as what the government can't do to us.

This is by design. As Virginia delegate Edmund Randolph noted: "In the draught of a fundamental constitution, two things deserve attention: 1. To insert essential principles only; lest the operations of government should be clogged by rendering those provisions permanent and unalterable, which ought to be accommodated to times and events; and 2. To use simple and precise language, and general propositions, according to the example of the...constitutions of the several states."[2] The American Constitution is built for endurance—not for pleasure or for speed—and indeed it has lasted, picking up the occasional amendment, for over two centuries of war and peace. Its genius is in its simplicity. It is the oldest constitution in the world, even though it belongs to one of the youngest nations.

And yet within its tenets, our Constitution includes intellectual property, something specific, value added, and extremely extraordinary for a society that was then ninety percent farmers. Among the legislature's limited enumerated powers, along with mentions of establishing post

---

2. *Supplement to Max Farrand's The Records of the Federal Convention of 1787*, James H. Hutson, editor (Yale University Press, 1987), 183.

offices and organizing militias, in Article I, Section 8, Clause 8, we are instructed: "The Congress shall have Power…To promote the Progress of Science and useful Arts, by securing for limited Times to Authors and Inventors the exclusive Right to their respective Writings and Discoveries." This simple sentence, which authorizes a national copyright and patent regime, is alternately known as the Intellectual Property Clause or the Progress Clause.

Whatever you call it, its implications have been larger for the economy of this country than the whole of the Constitution constituted together: In 2010, according to the United States Patent and Trademark Office, intellectual property was valued at $5.06 trillion annually, or thirty-five percent of our gross domestic product.[3] According to Richard Florida, thirty percent of American professionals—thirty-eight million people—are in the "creative class," compared to ten percent in 1900, fifteen percent in 1945, and a mere twenty percent in 1980.[4] In the two decades between 1980 and 2000, the United States created thirty million new jobs—as compared to five million in all of Europe—and much of this is attributable

3. Rebecca M. Blank and David J. Kappos, "Intellectual Property and the U.S. Economy: Industries in Focus," (United States Department of Commerce 2012), 3.

4. Richard Florida, *The Rise of the Creative Class: And How It's Transforming Work, Leisure, Community and Everyday Life* (Basic Books, 2002), 8-9.

to our investment in intellectual property.[5] While we are thought to be a service economy, we are actually a nation of "symbol manipulators"[6]—animators, web designers, physicists, choreographers, screenwriters, historians, couturiers, engineers, televangelists, televisionaries, technocrats, journalists, and, yes, attorneys. Perhaps the people who thrive the most in a world of ideas are intellectual property lawyers: Only five percent of patents have any commercial value,[7] but since 1992 the rate of patent litigation has more than doubled.[8]

Could the Founding Fathers and the Framers of the Constitution have envisioned this world?

To the modern mind, it seems an obvious inclusion—although many of the European constitutions drafted after World War II have no such thing. We are now so steeped in an idea-based economy—if not a whole life in the ether of cyberspace—that it makes retroactive sense that the Founders envisioned a future full of intellectual property. But at the time of the Constitutional Conven-

---

5. Charles Handy, "Tocqueville Revisited: The Meaning of American Prosperity," *Harvard Business Review* (January 2001), 6.

6. Justin Hughes, "Copyright and Incomplete Historiographies: Of Piracy, Of Propertization, And Thomas Jefferson," *Southern California Law Review* 79 (2006): 993, 1079.

7. Clara Jeffrey, "Intellectual Property Run Amok," *Mother Jones* (March/April 2006).

8. Michael J. Meurer and James Bessen, "The Patent Litigation Explosion," American Law & Economics Association Annual Meeting, Paper 57 (2005).

tion, in 1787, with nine out of ten Americans milking cows and literally reaping what they sowed, it was a supreme leap of faith to believe that there would ever be culture in this country, anything like literature and art, science and invention, anything that would demand and command copyright and patent.

But beyond that, even given that the Founding Fathers held such hopes—for plainly, they must have had high hopes—it is curious that intellectual property is in the Constitution: It could have later been enacted by statute, as part of Congress's powers under the Commerce Clause, which gives the legislature the right to regulate interstate and foreign trade. There's no particular reason that the Constitution, which otherwise contains few frills, should bother to make mention of something as luxurious to a nascent nation as intellectual property. James Madison, who, along with Charles Pinckney of South Carolina, is responsible for the inclusion of the Progress Clause, himself said it was "of inferior moment."[9]

And yet, there it is. As such, it made America. Because of intellectual property, we live in a democracy of ideas and not a plutocracy of provenance. Here, ingenuity is everything.

9. Bruce W. Bugbee, *Genesis of American Patent and Copyright Law* (Public Affairs Press, 1967), 125.

3

I often wonder if the Founding Fathers sat down in the pub over steins of ale, or at a dining room table over a hardy supper, and said to each other, *Let's start a country.* They must have been crazy: Seventy percent of businesses fail within a decade, so what chance has a startup nation got? They were bold. Obviously, history has taught us that nothing quite so revolutionary happened—while there was indeed an American Revolution, the evolution from colonies to states, from confederation to nation, was far more gradual—but there is plainly a miraculous nerve in the generation that begat America. It was not the work of the ordinary. As with the miracles of science, so with American history, by the time we're old enough to appreciate the intricacies, we've heard the stories of the Pilgrims and George Washington and Thanksgiving too many times since youth to be awestruck that it worked out at all. We think the Indians gave the settlers red corn, they all said *L'Chaim* and ate turkey and *voilà*! But of course, it took some doing. So it should be no surprise that beyond the ordinary success of getting the country going, the Founding Fathers had some aspirations to the exquisite.

They knew that to be a great nation, they had to become culturally competitive with the countries they'd left behind, like England and France. As poet Joel Barlow said to the Continental Congress in 1782: "A literary reputation is necessary in order to complete national character."[1] Said lexicographer Noah Webster, in a petition to the New York and Connecticut legislatures: "America must be as independent in literature as it is in Politics, as famous of arts as for arms."[2] Alexander Hamilton—the bastard out of Bermuda who founded *The New York Post*—wanted to see the country become part of the industrial world. As a founder of the Pennsylvania Society for the Encouragement of Manufactures and Useful Arts, and later as Secretary of the Treasury, Hamilton wished to hearten the kind of industrial invention that would eventually lead to "our world supremacy in technology."[3]

But why did the Founders decide to promote those ends through a copyright and patent system? Why not

1. Irah Donner, "The Copyright Clause of the U.S. Constitution: Why Did the Framers Include It With Unanimous Approval?" *American Journal of Legal History* 36 (1992): 361, 373.

2. Bugbee, *Genesis of American Patent and Copyright Law*, 108.

3. Karl B. Lutz, "A Clarification of the Patent Clause of the U.S. Constitution," *George Washington Law Review* 18 (1949): 50.

start an art academy or found a university? Why not patronize creativity by establishing the National Endowment for the Arts—an organization that did not come to be until 1965? Why not set up the National Science Foundation—as was finally done in 1950? In Europe, creativity and technological progress were commissioned by kings and patronized by nobles, so what gave the Framers the idea that they could leave something so important to market forces?

In establishing at the outset that all creative people would be at the mercy of the marketplace, the Framers invented a uniquely American form of creativity, which is commercial, widely appealing, and inevitably the stuff of empires. The Constitution is the force behind Hollywood and Silicon Valley, behind rock stars and rocket scientists, behind everything we love and everything we love to hate.

The Constitution made America.

4

opyright and patent demand that a creator or inventor make money by his wits: It is a popularity contest. It's paydirt or bust. The Intellectual Property Clause is an audience-oriented order: It is a grant of rights to promote progress for the public benefit. By comparison, in France, where the tradition of the auteur existed in court since at least the Renaissance, when the National Convention passed its post-Revolutionary copyright law in 1793, it was called a "Declaration of the Rights of Genius."[1] In the United States, you are a genius if people buy what you are selling.

This is not to say that the Founding Fathers lacked respect for artists: The Intellectual Property Clause was ratified by a unanimous vote with no debate. But the most beautiful painting is the one that fetches the highest price.

1. Carla Hesse, "The Rise of Intellectual Property, 700 B.C.-A.D. 2000: An Idea in the Balance," *Daedalus* (Spring 2002): 39.

A critical success with lousy box-office returns is not great at all until it makes money on-demand. And this goes back to the Constitution: Insofar as creativity was considered at all, it needed to cope with conditions of the market. This was partly pragmatic: They had no money. Setting up a patent regime provided "the desired pecuniary incentive to inventors," without any government investment per se, according to one historian: "This was a critical consideration for a new federal government that was contemplated to take over the state debts inherited from the Revolutionary War. Accordingly, from the perspective of delegates seeking to devise a form of governance for a fledgling, impecunious national government, granting limited-term exclusive rights to authors and inventors seemed the perfect solution to encouraging the progress of useful arts with the least expense."[2] When John Churchman, a young inventor, petitioned Congress for "patronage" funds, the "committee that looked into the matter reported that it was reluctant to recommend 'in the present deranged state of our finances, a precipitate adoption of a measure which would be attended by considerable expence.'"[3]

But this was also a matter of principle. This was the Age of Enlightenment, which brought with it many vogu-

2. Edward C. Walterscheid, "To Promote the Progress of Useful Arts: American Patent Law and Administration, 1787-1836," *Journal of the Patent and Trademark Office Society* 80 (1998): 11, 25.

3. *Ibid.*

ish philosophies that influenced the Framers. It is well known that as republicans, they believed in principles of equality: Every person was to achieve greatness or mediocrity or idiocy on his own merit and through his own efforts. "In a republican system," wrote the great historian Gordon Wood, "only talent would matter."[4] As Alexis de Tocqueville would observe, "The social condition of the Americans is eminently democratic; this was its character at the foundation of the colonies.…Even the germs of aristocracy were never planted in…the Union. The only influence which obtained there was that of intellect."[5] While real property is nobility's birthright, "Intellectual property is far more egalitarian," writes legal thinker Justin Hughes. "Of limited duration and obtainable by anyone, intellectual property can be seen as a reward, an empowering instrument, for the talented upstarts.…Intellectual property is often the propertization of what we call 'talent.' It tends to shift the balance toward the talented newcomers…by giving them some insurance against the predilections of the propertied class that had been their patrons."[6] Along with the Progress Clause, the Constitution provided, in Article I, Section 9, Clause 8: "No Title of Nobil-

4. Gordon Wood, *The Creation of the American Republic, 1776-1787* (University of North Carolina Press, 1998), 71.

5. Alexis de Tocqueville, *Democracy in America* (Everyman's Library, 1994), 46.

6. Justin Hughes, "The Philosophy of Intellectual Property," *Georgetown Law Journal* 77 (1988): 287, 291.

ity shall be granted by the United States: and no Person...shall, without the Consent of Congress, accept of any present, emolument, Office, or Title of any kind whatever from any King, Prince, or foreign State." Hence, any honors upon the arts or bestowed upon any variety of brilliance would, said Continental Army General Charles Lee, "be obtain'd without court favour, or the rascally talents of servility."[7]

This meant that the only available currency for achievement was currency itself. But a person of talent in the arts and sciences need not appeal to any wealthy family or scion thereof, because the republicans were enamored of another philosophy: laissez-faire capitalism. Adam Smith's *The Wealth of Nations* was published in 1776, the year that America declared its independence from England—so free markets and free colonies arrived together. Smith believed that by working in his own self-interest for his own wealth accumulation, each man could do the greatest good for a society's collective enrichment, and "the species of domestic industry which his capital can employ, and which the produce is likely to be of the greatest value, every individual, it is evident, can, in his local situation, judge much better than any statesman or lawgiver can do for him."[8] In other words, if you leave a man

7. Wood, *The Creation of the American Republic, 1776-1787*, 71.
8. Adam Smith, *The Wealth of Nations*, Book IV, Chapter 2 (Bartleby.com, 2001).

to choose his occupation, he will thrive and the economy will do the same: "[G]ive to every man that he shall enjoy the fruits of his own labor, [that] alone is sufficient to make any country flourish, notwithstanding these and twenty other absurd regulations of commerce...."[9] For Smith, if men proceed by "self-love," they will contribute to the good of all without intending to. The economy flourishes when people work hard at what they wish to do:

> As every individual, therefore, endeavors as much as he can both to employ his capital in the support of domestic industry, and so to direct that industry that its produce may be of the greatest value; every individual necessarily labors to render the annual revenue of the society as great as he can. He generally, indeed, neither intends to promote the public interest, nor knows how much he is promoting it. By preferring the support of domestic to that of foreign industry, he intends only his own security; and by directing that industry in such a manner as its produce may be of the greatest value, he intends only his own gain, and he is in this, as in many other cases, led by an invisible hand to promote an end which was no part of his intention. Nor is it always the worse for society that it was no part of it. By pursuing his own interest he frequently promotes that of society more effectually than when he really intends to promote it. I have never known much good done by those who affected to trade for the public good.[10]

9. *Ibid.*

This was the theory behind the Intellectual Property Clause: Let people create for pleasure and profit that it may be for the good of all. Seldom is virtue an incentive for quality when it comes to creativity. Money makes the world go around. And around and around.

10. *Ibid.*

5

Patent and copyright are not American inventions, but we have taken these legal forms to their logical limits: You can now get a patent for a tennis stroke or a copyright for the doodles that you sketch on the margins of your algebra textbook. That's the tension in American intellectual property law: You can exploit anything for profit if you can get away with it, but if you can't manage, you starve. This is the justice and the injustice in the system and what is fair and unfair in everything American: The market is not moral; it only values what sells. This is why creative people don't much like the Progress Clause: It accounts only for the audience, not for the artist or artisan. And even the successful creator is only temporarily credentialed with good fortune: It is hemlines up, hemlines down with no social insurance.

But life is unfair. If you get the feeling life is unfair, you are onto something. There is no justice in a meritocracy: The talented and the beautiful are rewarded disproportionately. And even the wicked get worse than they deserve. But what can you do? Go sue unfair. There is a huge class action lawsuit waiting to be filed against unfair.

As for the American souk: It trusts the wisdom of crowds. It is a terrible thing to be on the supply side in the age of Spotify, but on the receiving end, the cultural variety available now is variegated to infinity. There is nearly nothing you cannot see or hear or read on the World Wide Web in some form, from near and far. Somebody somewhere earns a cent or two every now and then because he wrote a song that lots of people like and because copyright still means something. *Something*: It is spread thin like oily, foul-tasting margarine on stale and crusty bread that is khaki with mold. The days of delicious creamy yellow butter are just a lingering lovely taste on the back of the tongue. The long tail is a short stick.

But what do we expect? In the beginning of human creativity, everything good was God-given, there was no patent on manna from heaven, no copyright on the blueprints of the Mishkan, and people entertained themselves by dancing with a statue of a golden calf at the foot of Mount Sinai. The Bible is of course all in the public domain; the Lord gave His words to Moses, gratis. "Alternatively, Plato thought that all ideas were held from birth in the mind, where they had transmigrated from earlier souls," writes Berkeley historian Carla Hesse. "Ancient Greeks did not think of knowledge as something that could be owned or sold. A scribe could be paid fees for his labor, an author awarded prizes for his achievement, but the gift of the gods was freely given....Socrates held the Sophists in contempt for charging fees for their learning."[1]

Hence, sophistry.

The first patent might well have been given for a recipe. The Sybarites, who are known for, yes, their sybaritic indulgence, enjoyed good food and great wine. Their civilization thrived until 510 B.C., and according to historian Athenaeus, writing about 200 B.C., "The Sybarites, having given loose to their luxury, made a law that...if any confectioner or cook invented any peculiar and excellent dish, no other artist was allowed to make this for a year; but he alone who invented it was entitled to all the profits to be derived from the manufacture of it for that time; in order that others might be induced to labour at excelling in such pursuits...."[2] Not quite the twenty-year patents that you get in the United States today, but a year was a lot in a life span of a chef of that epoch.

The Venetians are believed to have enacted the first patent law, possibly for the silk industry, in 1474.[3] The city-state's most famous patent recipient was Galileo Galilei, who in 1594 was granted a twenty-year monopoly

1. Hesse, "The Rise of Intellectual Property, 700 B.C.-A.D. 2000," 26.

2. Giles Sutherland Rich, "The 'Exclusive Right' Since Aristotle," *Federal Circuit Bar Journal* 14 (2004/2005): 217, 218.

3. Bugbee, *Genesis of American Patent and Copyright Law*, 25.

"privilege" for inventing a "machine for raising water and irrigating land with small expense and great convenience."[4] Between 1490 and 1600, Venice granted sixteen hundred of these patents for assorted new contraptions, and the republic thrived as a center for Mediterranean trade and treasure.[5] The practice soon spread to all major parts of Europe—especially ports and river areas like Naples, Genoa, Amsterdam, Cologne, Paris and London—as it became clear that rewarding men with exclusive rights to their inventions was a great spur to inventiveness.[6] "The first new institutions for the promotion of useful arts grew up in the circles of artisans themselves," explains patent attorney and historian Frank D. Prager, "where the inactivating influence of philosophy was at a minimum."[7]

In England, special royal monopoly grants were made to inventors, first by Elizabeth I and then by James I. These were gifts of patronage, mainly bestowed to allow a certain businessman control over the market for some staple commodity, like salt, iron, coal, paper, tin, vinegar, sulfur or even playing cards. In his *Commentaries on the Laws*

---

4. P. J. Federico, *Journal of the Patent Office Society* 8 (1926): 576.

5. Rich, "The 'Exclusive Right' Since Aristotle," 217, 219.

6. Frank D. Prager, "Historic Background and Foundation of American Patent Law," *American Journal of Legal History* 5 (1961): 309, 310.

7. F. D. Prager, "The Early Growth and Influence of Intellectual Property," *Journal of the Patent Office Society* 34 (1952): 106, 117.

of England, William Blackstone wrote: "These grants, whether of lands, honours, liberties, franchises, or aught besides, are contained in charters, or letters-patent, open letters, *literae patentes*: so called because they are not sealed up, but exposed to open view, with the great seal pendant at the bottom; and are usually directed or addressed by the king to all his subjects at large."[8] Only occasionally were these "letters-patent" used to induce artisans to come to England and introduce industries which did not previously exist on that side of the Channel, but for that purpose they were quite successful: Innovations in glassmaking, weaving, dyeing, mining, and smelting helped spur British manufacturing.[9]

In 1623, the Statute of Monopolies was enacted in England by Parliament, which created a proper foundation for a patent system in the Motherland. Section 6 of the act provided that "any declaration before mentioned shall not extend to any letters patent and grants of privilege for the term of fourteen years or under, hereafter to be made, of the sole working or inventors of such manner of new manufactures within this realm, to the true and first inventor of such manufactures, which others at the time of making of such letters patent and grants shall not

---

8. William Blackstone, *Commentaries on the Laws of England: In Four Books* (Childs & Peterson, 1860), 346.

9. Rich, "The 'Exclusive Right' Since Aristotle," 217, 221.

use, so as also they be not contrary to the law nor mischievous to the state...." In non-legalese, this means the original inventor of a novel contraption had a fourteen-year monopoly on his product, in the interest of encouraging what would come to be known as the Industrial Revolution.

The history of copyrights is more complex, as artists are less essential to commerce, more necessary for courtly amusement. Hence, authors would dedicate their books with baroque panegyrics to royals and noblemen, hoping that patronage would be the return on this purple prose of praise.[10] "[E]very philosopher at court becomes as much a slave as the first official of the crown," complained Voltaire as late as the eighteenth century.[11]

The situation also had a deleterious effect on the work itself: For every masterful masterpiece like the ceiling of the Sistine Chapel there was the bottomless kitsch of imitation Botticellis by lesser artists like Bicci, whose name is apparently aptly homonymous. Of course, so it is now and ever, Miles Davis and Miley Cyrus still occupy the same planet and the same playlist, but that's not the result of some deranged government or religious agenda. Back then, the European people were only allowed art and lit-

10. Hesse, "The Rise of Intellectual Property, 700 B.C.-A.D. 2000," 28.
11. Peter Gay, *The Enlightenment: The Science of Freedom* (W. W. Norton & Company, 1995), 63.

erature that was for the good of God and country: "The patronage system also served to embed public discourse firmly within the hierarchical order of medieval and early modern Europe," explains legal scholar Neil Weinstock Netanel. "During the Middle Ages, literature and art were commonly commissioned and controlled for purposes of public mystification. They were designed to impress upon their audience the dominant status of the patron, whether it be king, noble, or church. Later, within the framework of late Renaissance neoclassicism, the patronage system fostered a view of the arts as a 'gentleman's calling,' tailored to aristocratic tastes and far removed from common social experience and creative sensibility."[12]

Still, by pandering to patrons, many authors and artists managed to make a name for themselves, and by the time of the Renaissance, according to copyright historian Mark Rose, "readers began to treat books as expressions of individual personalities, and thus as distinctive and individualized."[13] But this individualism did not release creators from their noble golden cages: "[I]n the eighteenth century, writers and artists were [still] heavily dependent on royal, feudal, and church patronage for their livelihoods," says Netanel. "This dependency undermined the

12. Neil Weinstock Netanel, "Copyright and a Democratic Civil Society," *Yale Law Journal* 106 (1996): 283, 354.
13. Mark Rose, "Copyright and Its Metaphors," *UCLA Law Review* 50 (2002-2003): 1, 3.

expressive autonomy and thwarted the development of a vital, freethinking intelligentsia."[14] For the creators themselves, this may well have felt like a pact with the devil: "I live in hell and paint its pictures," wrote Michelangelo in a sonnet.[15]

Genius itself was understood as a gift from God, divinely inspired, such that in his *Warning to the Printers*, Martin Luther preached, "Freely have I received, freely have I given, and I want nothing in return." Luther's printing press was meant to disseminate brilliant ideas more widely, not more profitably.[16] European royalty had its own interests: It wished to censor what circulated and keep subversive thought out of the body politic and body public. The absolute monarchs of countries like England, Spain, and France granted exclusive publishing rights to particular printing guilds in exchange for concessions to their censorship regimes. The state and the stationers were unified in a business of keeping reading material "clean."[17]

William Caxton brought the printing trade to England in 1476, and instead of the occasional book for a wealthy patron, there were now runs on publications for a whole audience. Those involved in book production—printers,

14. Netanel, "Copyright and a Democratic Civil Society," 283, 354.

15. George Bull, *Michelangelo: A Biography* (Saint Martin's Press, 1998), 98.

16. Hesse, "The Rise of Intellectual Property, 700 B.C.-A.D. 2000," 28-9.

17. *Ibid.*, 30.

binders, sellers, illuminators—banded together in a guild called the Stationers' Company, chartered by Mary Tudor, with a monopoly on the industry. In return for this recognition from the Crown, the Stationers received national jurisdiction over publishing. The guild agreed to proscribe the circulation of seditious texts. "Rights to profit from a book derived not from property in ideas, but from a 'privilege' extended by royal grace alone," writes Hesse.[18] Thus, in 1587, an edict from the Star Chamber declared that any member could admit no tract to the Stationers' Company register unless it had been approved first by an official censor.[19] This is the famous British prior restraint that the Framers of the Constitution were responding to when they created the First Amendment.

Notably omitted from membership in the Stationers' Company were authors, who—rather like today—were not considered particularly essential to the publication process. Then, as now, they were mere content providers. "This arrangement on either side was not in the service of some overarching goal like rewarding creators or encouraging intellectual progress," comments copyright scholar Diane Zimmerman.[20] "An author might sell a manuscript to a licensed publisher for a one-time fee, but the real

18. *Ibid.*

19. Diane Leenheer Zimmerman, "It's an Original! (?): In Pursuit of Copyright's Elusive Essence," *Columbia Journal of Law and the Arts* 28 (2005): 187, 191-2.

20. *Ibid.*, 192.

material rewards for the composition of a book came from the anticipated royal or aristocratic patronage that might redound, indirectly, to the writer from its publication," explains Hesse. "Authors could not publish their own books, and unless they obtained a privilege in their own name, they were denied profits from the sale of their books. These went to the publishers alone. State license monopolies on texts, on technical inventions, and on the means of reproducing them successfully wedded the commercial interests of publishers, printers, and other technical entrepreneurs to the ideological needs of absolutist states to control the knowledge that circulated in their realms."[21] This was the case throughout Europe.

Nonetheless, in the eighteenth century, the reading public grew considerably, such that philosopher Immanuel Kant observed: "This incessant reading has become an almost indispensable and general requisite of life."[22] Daniel Defoe in England, Denis Diderot in France, and Gotthold Lessing in Germany were even trying to live as writers for hire, rather than as the pets of patrons.[23] Long before, there had come to be a notion of the novel as the offspring of an author's personal brilliance: In his prologue to *Don Quixote of La Mancha*, Miguel de Cer-

---

21. Hesse, "The Rise of Intellectual Property, 700 B.C.-A.D. 2000," 31.
22. *Ibid.*
23. *Ibid.*, 32.

vantes bids forgiveness that his protagonist is not "the handsomest, the liveliest, and the wisest [child] that could be conceived."[24] Cervantes's pursuer of windmills was birthed in 1604. Similarly, in 1644, in *Aereopagitica*, John Milton conceives of a great tome as "the precious lifeblood of a master spirit, embalmed and treasured up on purpose to a life beyond life." It could hardly be surprising then that by 1710, in his plea for an author's copyright, Daniel Defoe conceived of plagiarism and piracy as a form of kidnapping:

> A Book is the Author's Property, 'tis the Child of his Inventions, the Brat of his Brain; if he sells his Property, it then becomes the Right of the Purchaser; if not, 'tis as much his own, as his Wife and Children are his own—But behold in this Christian Nation, these Children of our Heads are seiz'd, captivated, spirited away, and carry'd into Captivity, and there is none to redeem them.[25]

Authors' pleas for their rights as creators might not have amounted to much without the Enlightenment and John Locke's concepts of property and ownership via labor:

> Though the Earth, and all inferior Creatures, be common to all Men, yet every Man has a Property in his own Person: this no Body has any Right to but himself. The Labour

24. Rose, "Copyright and Its Metaphors," 1, 3.
25. Daniel Defoe, "Miscellanea," *Defoe's Review* (Columbia University Press, 1938), 517.

of his Body, and the Work of his Hands, we may say, are properly his. Whatsoever then he removes out of the State that Nature hath provided, and left it in, he hath mixed his Labour with, and joined to it something that is his own, and thereby makes it his Property. It being by him removed from the common state Nature hath placed it in, it hath by this labour something annexed to it, that excludes the common right of other Men: for this Labour being the unquestionable Property of the Labourer, no Man but he can have a right to what that is once joined to, at least where there is enough, and as good, left in common for others.[26]

While no one could own an idea, once an author or artist added his creativity and labor, the ineffable, effervescent notions came to be his own. This was the philosophical justification for copyright: Just as a man could appropriate a tract of land from the commons by planting and plowing upon it, so thoughts became propertied in print by the ingenuity of some genius—or mere hack—who transformed them into something more by applying pen to paper. In the eighteenth century, the idea was that the words were worth more money than the book they were printed in, the page was more than paper. Yes, words are just words, but given over to Shakespeare, they become a sonnet or a play, and latter-day bards deserved to own their work.

26. John Locke, *Two Treatises of Government* (Kessinger Publishing, 2004), 12.

But not forever. In 1694, Locke sent a memo to Parliament proposing that "it may be reasonable to limit [the writers'] property to a certain number of years after the death of the author, or the first printing of the book, as, suppose, fifty or seventy years."[27] This is elementary in the twenty-first century, but three hundred years ago the idea that someone could take possession of something as slippery and elusive as the products of his intellect was slippery and elusive. While still a barrister in 1761, Justice Joseph Yates of the Court of the King's Bench argued that a published work was "like land thrown on a highway."[28]

Along with authors' wishes for recognition and remuneration, the reading public and its appetites for material grew during the eighteenth century. There was a large market for pirated editions as the public demanded cheaper copies than the monopolists would supply. "Government legislators sought to increase commerce and to encourage a more educated population within their realms," writes Hesse. "Foreign and provincial publishers—most notably in Scotland, Switzerland, and secondary French cities like Lyon—clamored against the perpetual monopolies of the London and Paris Book Guilds on the most lucrative books."[29] In the midst of competing

27. Mark Rose, "Nine-tenths of the Law: The English Copyright Debates and the Rhetoric of the Public Domain," *Law and Contemporary Problems* 66 (2003): 75, 78.

28. *Tonson v. Collins*, 96 Eng. Rep. 180, 185 (King's Bench, 1761).

interests, debate about the origin of ideas too emerged, and the possibility that all did not come freely from God started to seem possible. John Locke's theories became a sensible alternative, and authors came to seem more like true creators, because, as Netanel points out, "[f]reed from capricious and overbearing patrons, writers enjoyed a new broad latitude to choose their own subject matter and find their own voice."[30] By 1725, a report on copyright from the Paris booksellers urged, "the work produced by an author is 'the fruit of a labour that is personal to him, which he must have the liberty to dispose of at will.'"[31]

In 1710, Parliament passed the Statute of Anne, regarded as the first public copyright act. Until then, a license to publish was "copied" into a registry at the Stationers' Company guild, giving its members the exclusive "right" to publish a book—hence the word copyright. Because of this new parliamentary law, copyright would no longer belong to entrepreneurs—rather, creators would own it. Because of the Glorious Revolution of 1688, England had new liberties, including a far freer press: Seditious libel was not so much of a concern.

The Statute of Anne transformed "what historically had been the publishers' private law copyright into a pub-

29. Hesse, "The Rise of Intellectual Property, 700 B.C.-A.D. 2000," 33.

30. Netanel, "Copyright and a Democratic Civil Society," 283, 354.

31. Jon M. Garon, "Normative Copyright: A Conceptual Framework for Copyright Philosophy and Ethics," *Cornell Law Review* 88 (2003): 1278, 1296.

lic law grant."[32] The statute was subtitled "An Act for the Encouragement of Learning, By Vesting the Copies of Printed Books in the Authors or Purchasers of such Copies, during the Times therein mentioned." Ownership of rights in any book would belong to the author for a term of fourteen years, which could be renewed for another fourteen if the writer lived that long. As for already extant works, their copyright was a single term of twenty-one years. As Mark Rose points out, these figures "probably relate to ancient formulas having to do with emancipation. Seven years is the traditional term of an apprenticeship, a formula that is as old as the Book of Genesis. Twenty-one, the traditional age of majority, is three times seven. Implicit in the original copyright term, then, was the notion that, like a child, a protected work would eventually be emancipated."[33] Indeed, after the copyright expired, literary works were to become free for all, as part of the public domain.

32. L. Ray Patterson and Craig Joyce, "Copyright in 1791: An Essay Concerning the Founders' View of the Copyright Power Granted to Congress in Article I, Section 8, Clause 8 of the U.S. Constitution," *Emory Law Journal* 52 (2003): 909, 916.
33. Rose, "Copyright and Its Metaphors," 1, 14.

6

Copyright and patent were familiar to the Framers of the Constitution. Of the fifty-five men who gathered in Philadelphia for the Constitutional Convention, thirty-one were lawyers[1]—which is why it is incredible that it is such a simple document. As such, they would have known the legal life of England and kept up with Blackstone's writings. Eight had signed the Declaration of Independence, and two the Articles of Confederation. Forty had served in Congress, and more than forty had been in state government as chief executive, judge, or legislator.[2] They were the policy wonks of Colonial America.

These men would have been quite aware of the state constitutions and codes. Many states had their own copyright and patent acts, because they'd been encouraged to

---

1. Irah Donner, "The Copyright Clause of the U.S. Constitution: Why Did the Framers Include It With Unanimous Approval?" *American Journal of Legal History* 36 (1992): 361, 374.

2. Walterscheid, "To Promote the Progress of Science and Useful Arts," 1, 30.

pass them by a resolution of the Continental Congress on May 2, 1783:

> That it be recommended to the several States, to secure to the authors or publishers of any new books not hitherto printed, being citizens of the United States, and to their executors, administrators and assigns, the copy right of such books for a certain time not less than fourteen years from the first publication; and to secure to the said authors, if they shall survive the term first mentioned, and to their executors, administrators and assigns, the copy right of such books for another term of time not less than fourteen years, such copy or exclusive right of printing, publishing and vending the same, to be secured to the original authors, or publishers, their executors, administrators and assigns, by such laws and under such restrictions as to the several States may seem proper.

Joel Barlow agitated for this proclamation, pleading to Congress: "If the passing of statutes similar to [the Statute of Anne] were recommended…to the several states, the measure would undoubtedly be adopted, & the consequences would be extensively happy upon the spirit of the nation."[3] In response to Congress's urging, every state save Delaware enacted some kind of intellectual property

3. Patterson and Joyce, "Copyright in 1791," 909, 931.

act—sometimes for copyright, sometimes for patent, sometimes both: It cost them nothing.

Joel Barlow is an unlikely hero of intellectual property, because unlike copyright champion Noah Webster, Barlow's literary legacy is pretty shady. He is best known for the 1793 comic-epic poem "Hasty Pudding." Despite the Harvardian title, Barlow graduated from Yale after a brief stint at Dartmouth—and he was a brief-stint kind of guy. Barlow's life was more storied than his creations, as he ran a land-sale scam in France, inadvertently founded a town in Ohio, and, as consul to Algiers, negotiated a treaty in Tripoli with the Barbary pirates. Barlow was a plenipotentiary in Paris and a loafer in London, but he is best known for his time in Connecticut as one of the Hartford Wits. Nevertheless, Barlow's abolitionist poem, "The Prospect of Peace," is not up there with "John Brown's Body." *The Columbiad*, Barlow's rococo volume in neoclassical couplet, which tells the story of the man who discovered America while looking for India, has been described as "pompous"[4] and "sumptuous"[5] and just plain "bad."[6] But

4. *The Princeton Encyclopedia of Poetry and Poetics*, Roland Greene, Stephen Cushman, Clare Cavanagh, Jahan Ramazani, Paul F. Rouzer, Harris Feinsod, David Marno, Alexandra Slessarev, editors (Princeton University Press, 2012), 1,224.

5. Henry Augustin Beers, *The Connecticut Wits: And Other Essays* (Yale University Press, 1920), 27.

6. *The Library of Literary Criticism of English and American Authors,* vol. IV

Joel Barlow was there before the thirteen-state legislature, in 1783, on behalf of all authors.

Well before that, in 1641, the Massachusetts Bay Colony had a patent clause as part of its "Body of Liberties," which read: "No monopolies shall be granted or allowed amongst us, but of such new Inventions yt are prfitable to ye Countrie, & yt for a short time."[7] And in 1673, a full thirty-seven years before the Statute of Anne, Massachusetts passed a copyright law, although it placed ownership with the publisher, in this particular case a man named John Usher, who was granted title for "at least this seven years, unless he shall have sold them all before that time, [during which] there shall be no other or Au'ther impression made by any person thereof, in this jurisdiction, under the penalty this Court shall see cause to lay on any that shall adventure in that kind, beside making full satisfaction...for his charge and damage therein."[8]

Even before the Continental Congress made its 1783 resolution, in January of the same year Connecticut was the first state to pass a general copyright statute, entitled "An Act for the Encouragement of Literature and Genius." In its preamble, the Connecticut law explains that "it is

(1785-1824), Charles Wells Moulton (assisted by a corps of able contributors), editor (Charles Malkan, 1910), 575.

7. http://www.archive.org/stream/coloniallawsofma1890mass/coloniallawsofma1890mass_djvu.txt.

8. *Ibid.*

perfectly agreeable to principles of natural equity and justice, that every author should be secured in receiving the profits that may arise from the sale of his works, and such security may encourage men of learning and genius to publish their writings; which may do honor to their country, and service to mankind."[9] It was soon followed by copyright acts in Massachusetts and Maryland. The congressional resolution brought along the nine other states. Massachusetts set the tone for the others—its statute was copied exactly by New Hampshire and Rhode Island. The preamble reads:

> Whereas the improvement of knowledge, the progress of civilization, the public weal of the community, and the advancement of human happiness, greatly depend on the efforts of learned and ingenious persons in the various arts and sciences: As the principal encouragement such persons can have to make great and beneficial exertions of this nature, must exist in the legal security of the fruits of their study and industry to themselves; and as such security is one of the natural rights of all men, there being no property more peculiarly a man's own than that which is procured by the labor of his mind....

The Massachusetts law itself made copyright length

9. B. Zorina Khan, *The Democratization of Invention: Patents and Copyrights in American Economic Development, 1790-1920* (Cambridge University Press, 2005), 234.

twenty-one years and required that two copies of each book be deposited in the library of the "university at Cambridge," meaning Harvard. Perhaps the zealous nature of the statute's introduction can be explained by Massachusetts's state constitution, authored with great style by John Adams, which includes its own version of the Progress Clause:

> **The Encouragement of Literature**, etc. Wisdom, and knowledge, as well as virtue, diffused generally among the body of the people, being necessary for the preservation of their rights and liberties; and as these depend on spreading the opportunities and advantages of education in the various parts of the country, and among the different orders of the people, it shall be the duty of legislatures and magistrates, in all future periods of this commonwealth, to cherish the interests of literature and the sciences, and all seminaries of them; especially the university at Cambridge, public schools and grammar schools in the towns; to encourage private societies and public institutions, rewards and immunities, for the promotion of agriculture, arts, sciences, commerce, trades, manufactures, and a natural history of the country; to countenance and inculcate the principles of humanity and general benevolence, public and private charity, industry and frugality, honesty and punctuality in their dealings; sincerity, good humor, and all social affections, and generous sentiments among the people.

John Adams would, of course, eventually become second

president of the whole country and was one of the great men of the early republic. He was also a nerd extraordinaire, given to such affectations as wearing a sword in a hip holster when he stood before Congress, and for such reasons was something of a failure as a leader but incomparable as a writer. The Massachusetts constitution is perhaps the most eloquent of those of all the states, and the first to set forth the idea that good civic life and virtue are encouraged by the humanities and arts. "[L]iterature and knowledge are regarded as a necessary means to achieve democratic ideals of protecting 'rights and liberties'," argues law professor Michael D. Birnhack. "This is the first place that we can note that knowledge is assigned a direct political purpose. It states that literature and the sciences are not cherished as ends in themselves, but as means to achieve democratic values."[10] It is the effect on the audience—not the pleasure of the artist that matters: This is the onset of service with a smile.

But far more revolutionary: This was the beginning of mass culture at the beginning of a nation. From the start, it was understood that the stuff was for everybody. Never in America were the arts meant to be exclusive. While the democratization of culture was beginning in Europe, it was the natural state of affairs in the states of America.

10. Michael D. Birnhack, "The Idea of Progress in Copyright Law," *Buffalo Intellectual Property Law Journal* 1 (2001): 3, 30.

7

Before we explore this further—because this is the start of the most wildly exuberant invention ever—popular culture—I want to bring up an entirely different subject: moving. As in moving from one place to another. From home to home, from town to town, from city to city, or even just from block to block. Or, in the case of the founding generation of Americans, from continent to continent. Now, as anyone who has ever packed boxes, duct-taped crates, rented a U-Haul truck, or hired a crew of burly Israeli men from Forest Hills knows: Moving is hell. This is why the all-knowing humorist Dave Barry has just one rule about moving: "Don't do it!"[1] Nonetheless, in 2012 some thirty-six million Americans moved, which is nearly twelve percent of the population.[2] While this is normal here, this is not true in the rest of the world, unless

1. Dave Barry, *Homes and Other Black Holes* (Ballantine Books, 1988), 51.
2. https://www.census.gov/newsroom/releases/archives/mobil-
   ity_of_the_population/cb13-192.html.

you are yourself an immigrant, mostly not a happy thing to be. In fact, as the current dialogue indicates, it is mostly a despised thing, and it involves a lot of schlepping of belongings and bodies from place to place. Even now, an immigrant is an extreme person. No matter how bad circumstances are in your native country, regardless of the death threat, complacency and entropy means most people will stay put amid famine and genocide. Anyone who crosses deserts and mountains and oceans and borders because life means more to him than stillness is brave. Never disrespect an immigrant. The brilliance of America is the constant regeneration of this daring population. And it is how this country started. And keeps renewing.

Whatever brought the colonists here, they came not on the now-defunct Concorde, not even flying tourist class on a British Airways 767, but on boats and ships, on high seas and low, seeking fortune and freedom—and they cannot have been happy where they were before. England had to have been extremely disagreeable. I say this not as a reader of history, but as a mover of furniture: my own. And it's not fun. And in the seventeenth century, people did not move and migrate much: You were born and you died in the same village, most likely in the same house. This was so much the case that the invention of the bicycle in 1818 is said to have dramatically stirred up the gene pool by increasing the courting radius and allowing marriage and mating to occur between couples from different towns.[3] Imagine that: A two-wheeled vehicle was more thrilling than Tinder. Imagine the incredible dullness of the eighteenth century: If you think it's annoying to wait for the next season of *House of Cards*, just think of a time when the big excitement was a change in the weather. Nothing ever happened back then. No one left his village. There was work and sleep and church on Sunday and the same people all the time. So those who traveled overseas to live were the outliers of history. They were the outliers of everything.

Certainly among the ragtag team of settlers who came to America in the early rounds there were noblemen seeking adventure, governors serving royalty, businessmen wanting a bigger bang for the buck, sensuous swashbucklers—but there had to be a huge assortment of lonesome losers with nothing better to do than pray that the plague strike anywhere but here. To start with, this was quite a mess. Anyone who has been through first grade and has heard the story of the first Thanksgiving knows this. History is written by the winners, and most of the primary documents we look at from that time are the lucid texts of the Founders, but the colonies were as turbulent as the epicenter of the San Francisco earthquake of 1906—and California was not even part of this country to begin with.

3. Bowen H. McCoy, *Living Into Leadership: A Journey in Ethics* (Stanford University Press, 2007), 198.

Starting a state is a crackpot undertaking, and while we revere Washington and his peers, we cannot forget that they must have been crazy, as were all the people who came here, thinking for whatever desperate reason that it was a good idea.

And it was. It was a great idea. Also: crazy.

(A 2006 study by psychiatrists at Duke University Medical Center study found that forty-nine percent of American presidents between 1776 and 1974 were mentally ill.)[4]

Gordon Wood's masterpiece, *The Creation of the American Republic, 1776-1787*, reads like a study of insanity. On the first page, Professor Wood makes clear that the American Revolution is inexplicable: "[T]he sources of its force and its momentum appeared strangely unaccountable...the Americans knew they were probably freer and less burdened with cumbersome feudal and hierarchical restraints than any part of mankind in the eighteenth century."[5] Then, turning to contemporaneous sources, Wood notes that "[n]ever in history...had there been so much rebellion with 'so little real cause'...'the most wanton and unnatural rebellion that ever existed.' The Americans'

---

4. Haley Hoffman, "Study posits presidents had mental illness," *The Duke Chronicle* (February 21, 2006). http://www.dukechronicle.com/articles/2006/02/22/study-posits-presidents-had-mental-illness.

5. Gordon Wood, *The Creation of the American Republic, 1776-1787* (University of North Carolina Press, 1998), 3.

response was out of all proportion to the stimuli: 'The Annals of no Country can produce an Instance of so virulent a Rebellion, of such implacable madness and Fury, originating from such trivial Causes, as those alledged by these unhappy people.'"[6]

By Wood's reckoning, the American Revolution is an act of collective lunacy—in the genus of philosophy, in the species of what Edmund Randolph called "theoretic reasoning."[7] The theology of freedom had spread throughout the land, a belief so huge that eventually men were willing to take up arms to defend an idea: It was mind over matter. This was not France, where the masses were starving when they stormed the barricade; this was America, where they could afford to toss tea into the Atlantic out of outrage. This was the foreign policy version of no-fault divorce: America had fallen out of love with Great Britain. Based on the variety of "theoretic reasoning" that drove Thomas Paine to write *Common Sense*—and many Americans paid heed—the British colonies worked their way into declaring independence and then armed themselves to defend liberty. Professor Wood read thousands of pamphlets written and distributed in the colonies in the buildup to the American Revolution, and he concludes that this agitprop worked. It was as bad as pundits scream-

6. *Ibid.*, pages 3-4.
7. *Ibid.*, 4.

ing on Fox News today: It radicalized the polity against the Empire, even though it was an ocean away, and hands off. Obsession, not oppression, was the force for armed conflict.

This might be a thing of beauty. Perhaps the colonists could rightly say, "the present is an age of philosophy, and America the empire of reason."[8] If it is ever possible to be reasonable when picking a fight: All of America's wars are a choice, because we are an island republic far from the madding crowd. So whenever we go to battle we are highly principled or quite the opposite. Even the war that created this nation could have been invented by PhDs testing grand theories of government. Hysteria for freedom and passion for independence infiltrated the colonies like a wildfire virus and brought revolution. America was born of desire.

We are all guilty of the belief that sex—or at least hot sex—was invented in 1967. Or 1981. Or 1993. Or last year, if you're a teenager. It's hard for the postmodern mind to reckon that wild times might have been long ago, maybe even before Woodstock or Studio 54 or—or yesterday. Perhaps people were as crazy in late eighteenth-century America as any version of craziness that we are accustomed to now. Perhaps it was its own Age of Aquarius in

8. Richard Buel, Jr., *Joel Barlow: American Citizen in a Revolutionary World* (Johns Hopkins University Press, 2011), 95.

a way that even we could recognize, if we thought of it that way. Perhaps, as Bob Dylan said of a more recent era, "There was music in the cafes at night/And revolution in the air." It might be advantageous to look at the American founding as a project of people not in their right minds.

This is a land of those not happy in the Old World. It is a new world. It is a place for people who lived badly by the rules of the royals, badly enough that they could be talked into lending life and limb to the cause of getting rid of them. The Founding Fathers had to know that if this country could be led to revolution by pamphlets, the potential for creativity was out there. Despite the talent for nothing but farming, people here invented their own idea of how life should be. This is not a center of convention. This is still a nation always discontented, and chasing the next new thing to make it better. And the newborn country was so obviously a special place that by 1807, Mercy Otis Warren had already written the three-volume *History of the Rise, Progress, and Termination of the American Revolution*. While early America was hardly a happy home for an artist or artisan—or probably much of anything—it was meant to be hospitable to precocious, preposterous creativity and creation. There had to be money in this madness somewhere down the line. If human beings might someday fly rockets to the moon, they would be launched from America.

Right away, this country made the making of things a

way to make money. A life of living by one's wits is central to the conception of American greatness. It is possible for anyone clever to clean up in this economy, because the system is good to those who are good at something. A meritocracy is not fair at all: It rewards the talented, the brilliant, and the beautiful, who are already lucky. But this is the American way. This is the incentive to the inventive. Thomas Alva Edison and his laboratory would eventually patent 1,093 inventions, including the movie camera, the phonograph, and the light bulb. At age twenty-one, with no money and no nothing, the Wizard of Menlo Park sighed, "I may live to be fifty. I have so much to do and life is so short. I am going to hustle!"[9] Because of the Intellectual Property Clause of the Constitution, America is amenable to genius hustlers and hucksters. Through their insane rebellion, Americans showed they were up for anything, and the Constitution included a provision for gifted children, for daring thinkers. This country has been bound for glory or the ditch, which is really the nature of all popular culture, of the Hollywood blockbuster, of the great American Dream.

9. Louise Egan and Louise Betts, *Thomas Edison: The Great American Inventor* (Barron's Educational Series, 1987), 58.

8

The Progress Clause is phrased very precisely. It gives Congress a mandate "to promote the Progress of Science and the useful Arts," and then it instructs them to do so "by securing to Authors and Inventors for limited Times the exclusive right to their Discoveries and Writings." This is "A Most Unusual Clause"[1] in that, unlike the other eighteen powers enumerated to the legislature, it not only tells Congress what to do, but also how to do it: The senators and representatives are tasked with promoting progress, and they are specifically told to establish patent and copyright. They are not given specific instructions on how to go about regulating commerce, which has caused a great deal of contretemps in the courts in ensuing centuries. They can also pretty much arrange a postal system harum-scarum and coin (or paper) money in whatever manner they see fit. But when it comes to forwarding

1. Walterscheid, "To Promote the Progress of Science and Useful Arts," 1.

inventions and ideas, Congress is limited to giving out exclusive rights for a period of time to those who come up with anything ingenious.

While the legislature would early on establish the Library of Congress—within the capital in 1800—and eventually, after World War II, the federal government would find its way to funding large undertakings in the sciences and humanities—hence the military-industrial complex—to begin with, the United States threw creativity to the marketplace. There was no such thing as a secretary of the arts in the president's cabinet, there was no department of literature in the administration, and there was no office for the advancement of inventive endeavors in the government bureaucracy—insofar as there was any bureaucracy. In France, the cabinet has contained a minister of culture since Charles de Gaulle established such a thing in 1959, but the idea that the government must mind the arts as a patron for national prestige has existed there since at least the sixteenth century. Almost every nation in Europe—including Macedonia and Bulgaria, all of Scandinavia, and all of our Western allies—has a cultural ministry, as do Iran and Afghanistan: It is one of the first posts established in the process of civilization. Not the United States.

The Founders were giving credit to the audience. In fact, this was the invention of the audience. Yes, in England people could see Shakespeare performed at the

Globe, but it was at the pleasure of the Queen. Culture in Europe was created for the courts of kings, who anted up large sums, or else in Italy there were noble families like the Medicis and gangsters like the Catholic Church putting up the money for artists. Here the idea was everyone would buy a ticket or purchase a copy, and *voilà!*—fun. Everyone pays a little and gets back a lot. Culture is as democratic as government. When it comes to taste, the people rule. Their choices, and not those of some wiser arbiters, are to be trusted to decide on what is worthy of making it out into the world. Therefore, only art that is truly popular, and inventions that are actually useful, stand a chance.

By keeping government out of creativity, the Founding Fathers hoped to create something sorely lacking in the Europe they left behind: civil society. Civil society is that which thrives in public spaces, in the lives of townships and urbanscapes, among villagers and city dwellers, in the organizations they form that cohere communities. It is comprised of newspapers and magazines, dance troupes and theater companies, literary reviews and city symphonies, museums and galleries, science centers and opinion journals, trade unions and artisan guilds, reading groups and sports clubs, churches and synagogues, libraries and lyceums—anything that keeps people exchanging views, alive and lively, any centripetal cultural force that ensures that the center will hold. By the time the

Constitution was composed, the Framers knew that, provided with an enabling legal framework, the people could be trusted to create culture.

The Founding Fathers were virtuous and serious men, and their vision was not of a civil society centered on the gyrations of Elvis Presley's hips, or on the sinking ship in *Titanic*. Could they have imagined that Kanye West would want to pack it all in to design hotels? They did not see Jay-Z performing "Picasso Baby" as if holding court at the Pace Gallery. They did not contemplate Gawker. They did not live in a land of millions of Beliebers. No, not at all: The Framers had purer purposes. They wanted more historic novels, books of law, encyclopediae of philosophy. Perhaps they hoped that portrait painters might eventually no longer feel a need to go to Europe to establish a reputation or to receive academic training. Perhaps they wanted the occasional night out, and hoped for some decent theater now and again, some Shakespeare in the Park.

They had no idea what they started.

By referring to Samuel Johnson's *A Dictionary of the English Language* from the Founders' time, we can know what kind of "Progress" the Framers were trying to promote. *Progress* is itself defined, much as it would be today, as "course; procession; passage; advancement; motion forward; intellectual improvement; advancement in knowledge; proficience; removal from one place to another; a journey of state; a circuit."[2] One scholar points out that newspapers of the time frequently used the term "progress" to describe the spread of fire or an illness, and the forward movement of a band of armed men or ravenous insects[3]—but it was mostly a positive term: One of the most popular books was John Bunyan's *The Pilgrim's Progress*, published in 1678, an inspirational text.

While progress had much the same meaning in the Framers' era as it does today, *Science* was something else entirely: "knowledge; certainty grounded on demonstration; art attained by precepts, or built on principles; any art or species of knowledge; one of the seven liberal arts—grammar, rhetorick, logick, arithmetick, musick, geometry, astronomy."[4] Therefore, "science" meant almost any field of knowledge—or subject of a nonfiction book or article. As for *useful Arts*: Something is useful if it is "convenient; profitable to any end; conducive or helpful to any purpose; valuable for use"[5]; and it is an art if it has "the power of doing something not taught by nature," but it

2. Samuel Johnson, John Walker, Robert S. Jameson, *A Dictionary of the English Language* (W. Pickering, 1828), 573.

3. Malla Pollack, "What Is Congress Supposed to Promote?: Defining Progress in Article 1, Section 8, Clause 8 of the United States Constitution, or Introducing the Progress Clause," *Nebraska Law Review* 80 (2001): 754, 799.

4. Johnson, Walker, *A Dictionary of the English Language*, 641.

5. *Ibid.*, 806.

might also be "a science, as the liberal arts; a trade; artfulness; skill; dexterity."[6] So the "useful arts" would be inventions—though the meaning includes anything produced by talent.

As for the recipient of a patent or a copyright: An *Author* is not simply a creator of texts, he is "[t]he first beginner or mover; the efficient; he that affects or produces anything; the first writer of anything; a writer in general."[7] And an *Inventor* does not merely create, he also discovers, he is "[a] finder out of something new; a contriver; a framer."[8] *Writings* are what an attorney might be engaged with, as the singular is defined as "a legal instrument, as the writings of an estate; a composure; a book; a written paper of any kind."[9] A *Discovery*, understood as it is now, is "[t]he act of finding anything hidden; the act of revealing or disclosing any secret"—so it is insight where there was previously none.

It seems that Congress has the right to promote whatever it wishes. Secrets and sensations, art and arithmetic, everything a person might possibly come up with is encompassed somewhere in there. Expectations were high

6. *Ibid.*, 44.
7. *Ibid.*, 53.
8. *Ibid.*, 404.
9. *Ibid.*, 828.

and open. The Intellectual Property Clause gave legal license to lush creativity.

9

It is often assumed that Thomas Jefferson must have had something to do with the Progress Clause. This is possibly because, as the Secretary of State, he was the first administrator of the first patent office. Also, a letter of his is quoted in the 1966 Supreme Court case *Graham v. John Deere Company*, which explicates the nonobviousness standard in patents; Jefferson has been cited in intellectual property decisions ever since. And when the United States Patent and Trademark Office opened its new headquarters in Alexandria, Virginia in 2004, it was christened the Thomas Jefferson Building. So there is all that.

But it's something else: We like to believe that all good things from the American Revolution have something to do with Thomas Jefferson. Or that all good things ever have something to do with him. He's the cool one. He's the groovy patriarch. He has red hair. He is terribly handsome. He knows fine wine. He speaks six languages. He lives in Paris. He is a self-taught architect. He is founder of the University of Virginia. He loves beautiful women and he wrecks homes. He has that whole Sally Hemings thing going on, which seems to be a love story, so he is into interracial dating long before such things were done. And he wrote the Declaration of Independence, which is as good as it gets, and the rest of his opus is quite something. Thomas Jefferson is memorable because he is so cool. And because he is such a great writer. But he is such a great writer because he is so cool.

Still, insofar as Jefferson had anything to do with the Intellectual Property Clause—and mind you, he was in France at the time of the Constitution's construction—it was mostly to oppose its existence. As one scholar put it, Jefferson's ideology of intellectual property has produced "pseudohistory,"[1] and as another has written, "Jefferson had nothing whatever to do with the drafting of the Constitution and never set forth any interpretation of the [Progress Clause]."[2] The known and knowable truth is probably best summed up by a third scholar: "Leaving aside the fact that Jefferson, being a minister to France, did not attend the convention, his correspondence with Madison while the Constitution was pending ratification

1. Kenneth Burchfiel, "Revising the 'Original' Patent Clause: Pseudohistory in Constitutional Construction," *Harvard Journal of Law and Technology* 2 (1989): 155.

2. Walterscheid, *The Nature of the Intellectual Property Clause: A Study In Historical Perspective* (William S. Hein Publishing, 2002), ix.

reveals that he would have left the Intellectual Property Clause out."[3]

When Jefferson was minister, in 1787, a certain Monsieur L'Hommande approached him in Paris. The Frenchman had invented a better method of preserving flour, and had hopes that the American government might want to purchase rights to his technique. Jefferson's response expressed his views toward such arrangements:

> But I am not authorized to avail my country of it by making any offer for its communication. Their policy is to leave their citizens free, neither restraining nor aiding them in their pursuits. Though the interposition of government in matters of invention has its use, yet it is in practice so inseparable from abuse, that they think better not to meddle with it. We are only to hope, therefore, that those governments that are in the habit of directing all the actions of their subjects, by particular law, may be so far sensible of the duty they are under of cultivating useful discoveries, as to reward you amply for yours, which is among the most interesting to humanity.[4]

Of course, Jefferson was correct that at the time, under the Articles of Confederation, the American government

3. Dotan Oliar, "Making Sense of the Intellectual Property Clause: Promotion of Progress as a Limitation on Congress's Intellectual Property Power," *Georgetown Law Journal* 94 (2006): 1771, 1786.

4. Thomas Jefferson, *The Writings of Thomas Jefferson*, vol. 20 (issued under the auspices of the Thomas Jefferson Memorial Association of the United States, 1904), 255.

did not issue patents. And though the patent power existed in individual states, and he might have directed L'Hommande to apply to each, this would not have been sensible to Jefferson's sensibilities, because he was a thoroughgoing anti-monopolist.

Jefferson's antipathy toward monopolies developed after he had witnessed the effects of the French cartel on the tobacco trade, and of the agrarian lobby known as the Farmers-General on all of agriculture.[5] There was also, throughout the states, an anti-monopoly sentiment because so many corporations had been granted exclusive privileges in the colonies by the crown: Although the Boston Tea Party was a protest against taxation without representation, it was also a plaint against the imposition of the British East India Company. Consequently, the 1776 constitution of Maryland contained the provision "[t]hat monopolies are odious, contrary to the spirit of a free government, and the principles of commerce; and ought not to be suffered"; North Carolina's declared "[t]hat perpetuities and monopolies are contrary to the genius of a free State, and ought not to be allowed." To Jefferson, who continued to associate patents with a royal grant of privilege, intellectual property was no different from any other monopoly and so he viewed it as an "embarrassment."[6]

5. Walterscheid, *The Nature of the Intellectual Property Clause*, 5.

After James Madison posted a draft of the Constitution to him, Jefferson responded with satisfaction, but added: "I will now tell you what I do not like. First, the omission of a bill of rights, providing clearly and without the aid of sophism, for freedom of religion, freedom of the press, protection against standing armies, restriction of monopolies, the eternal and unremitting force of the habeas corpus laws and trials by jury in all matters of fact triable by the laws of the land."[7] He made no specific comment on the Progress Clause. Jefferson was to get his wished-for bill of rights—but until the Sherman Antitrust Act of 1890 and the Clayton Antitrust Act of 1914, the federal government took no stand against monopoly.

After the Constitution was ratified in 1788, Jefferson again corresponded with his friend Madison, this time to "rejoice," and to share his views on intellectual property, noting, "It is better…to abolish standing armies in time of peace, and Monopolies in all cases, than not to do it in any."[8] Jefferson added in a later missive: "The saying there shall be no monopolies, lessens the incitement to ingenuity, which is spurred by the hope of a monopoly for a limited time, as of fourteen years; but the benefit of even

6. Jefferson, *The Writings of Thomas Jefferson*, vol. 20, 335.

7. *Ibid.*, vol. 17-18, vii.

8. Thomas Jefferson, *The Works of Thomas Jefferson* (G.P. Putnam's Sons, 1904), 427.

limited monopolies is too doubtful to be opposed to that of their general suppression."[9]

Several months later, Madison replied:

> With regard to Monopolies, they are justly classed among the greatest nuisances in Government. But is it clear that as encouragement to literary works and ingenious discoveries, they are not too valuable to be wholly renounced? Would it not suffice to reserve in all cases a right to the public to abolish the privilege at a price to be specified in the grant of it? Is there not also infinitely less danger of this abuse in our Governments than in most others? Monopolies are sacrifices of the many to the few. Where the power is in the few it is natural for them to sacrifice the many to their own partialities and corruptions. Where the power, as with us, is in the many, not the few, the danger cannot be very great that the few will be thus favored. It is much more to be dreaded that the few will be unnecessarily sacrificed to the many.[10]

Jefferson remained committed to his "[belief] that the destiny of the United States resided primarily in its agricultural production rather than in any manufacturing base."[11] Somehow, he spent tons of time in Paris but remained preternaturally bucolic in his American dreaminess. As

9. *Ibid.*, 98.

10. James Madison, *Classics of American Political and Constitutional Thought* (Hackett Publishing, 2007), 529.

11. Walterscheid, *The Nature of the Intellectual Property Clause*, 8.

such, notes Justin Hughes, Jefferson "had a relatively modest impact on early American economic strategy....As an economist, Jefferson has usually been considered inconsistent, naïve, or simply wrong."[12] But at long last, in 1789, as a concession to his friend James Madison, Jefferson expressed a wish that the proposed Bill of Rights might include the following provision: "Monopolies may be allowed to persons for their own productions in literature, and their own inventions in the arts for a term not exceeding ___ years, but for no longer term, and for no other purpose."[13]

As the evaluator of inventions and assigner of rights, Thomas Jefferson eventually became a fan of the patent. After the first patent act was passed in 1790, when Jefferson became administrator in his role as Secretary of State, he even exclaimed: "An act of Congress authorizing the issuing of patents has given a spring to invention beyond my conception! Being an instrument in granting the patents, I am acquainted with their discoveries. Many of them are indeed trifling, but there are some of great consequence which have been proved by practice, and others if they stand the same proof will produce great effect."[14]

12. Justin Hughes, "Copyright and Incomplete Historiographies: Of Piracy, Propertization, and Thomas Jefferson," *Southern California Law Review* 79 (2006): 993, 1032.

13. Jefferson, *The Writings of Thomas Jefferson*, vol. 20, 451.

14. Thomas Jefferson, *The Writings of Thomas Jefferson: Autobiography, Correspon-

Among the patents Jefferson handed out were those for improvements in the milling of flour and meal, for steam navigation, for an easy method of rendering seawater potable, and for sawing and polishing stone. One of the last exclusive rights that Jefferson granted was to be his most important: the patent for Eli Whitney's cotton gin. In his correspondence with Whitney, Jefferson again referred to "embarrassment," but in this case, it was the shame of a cotton planter "clearing the cotton of the seed." As a farmer of that crop, Jefferson told Whitney, "I feel a considerable interest in the success of your invention for family use."[15] Jefferson knew a good thing when he saw one: Even today the United States is the largest exporter of cotton in the world.

In 1807, President Thomas Jefferson even praised intellectual property. In a letter to Oliver Evans, contraptor of the gristmill and the refrigerator, Jefferson waxes ebullient about the "utility a society derives from an invention." He concludes that "[c]ertainly an inventor ought to be allowed the right to the benefit of his invention for a certain time...Nobody wishes more than I do that ingenuity should receive a liberal encouragement." [16]

dence, Reports, Messages, Addresses, and Other Writings, Official and Private (H. W. Derby, 1859), 158.

15. *Jefferson Himself: The Personal Narrative of a Many-Sided American*, Bernard Mayo, editor (University of Virginia Press, 1988), 178.

16. Jefferson, *The Writings of Thomas Jefferson*, vol. 20, 200-2.

It's surprising then that Jefferson objected so vehemently to the ownership of ideas in the first place. This is yet another difficult thing for the twenty-first century mind to grasp: What the devil has intellectual property to do with monopoly? While we have some understanding that it is an antitrust violation when Microsoft Windows appears to appear on every computer, the lone inventor with a brilliant idea that makes the world a better place hardly feels like a monopolist—even if that was once Bill Gates. To us, a monopoly is the imposition of some single supplier of a necessary commodity on the market—or else it's a cartel of businesses acting in concert to set prices. Withholding your own unique idea is surely your right, and demanding a flow of revenue from such a thing, if consumers desire it, simply seems just. For that matter, to consider the case of a near-contemporary of Jefferson, surely James Fenimore Cooper was meant to turn a profit when *The Last of the Mohicans* was published in 1826—there's no way to explain how royalties on a book that would not exist but for the author could be construed as a monopoly. Short of returning to a patronage system—which is pre-American—there is no substitute for intellectual property.

10

Academia is now the focal point of the debate about intellectual property. Or else it's hysterical proclamations in 140 characters on Twitter when SOPA—the Stop Online Piracy Act—is up for a vote in Congress. The predominant position is that rights are much too strong, that the twenty-year length of a patent—and the life-plus-seventy-years length of a copyright, along with the hoarding of copyrights by large corporations[1]—is well beyond what the Framers ever intended. Intellectuals believe that the idea was to wrest the work of talented people out of their minds with adequate incentives, and get it into the public domain as quickly as possible. Most scholars argue that the Progress Clause is user-friendly, not creator-oriented, but that the legislation it has inspired is mostly too

1. U.S. Copyright Office, *Circular 1: Copyright Basics*, 5-6.
   http://www.copyright.gov/circs/circ01.pdf. (For a work by a corporation, "the duration of copyright will be 95 years from publication or 120 years from creation, whichever is shorter.")

advantageous to owners and therefore damaging to the future—whatever that may be. The conversation about intellectual property in the age of the Internet is an empire of the senseless. No one knows how to monetize anything correctly: These are the days of heaven only knows. "According to an organization called Tru Optik, as many as ten billion files, including movies, television shows, and games, were downloaded in the second quarter of [2014]," writes Louis Menand in *The New Yorker*. "Tru Optik estimates that approximately ninety-four percent of those downloads were illegal."[2]

Google, which at last count had sixteen lobbying groups to convince people that free is where it's at, always comes out ahead in this mess. Google values its own intellectual property very highly—just ask opposing counsel—but loves a free web. And bless them for doing what corporations have always done: Being evil while telling everyone else not to be. This is how big business makes big profits, and it is more apple-pie American than selling snake oil and claiming it is an elixir. Whatever Google is selling, all of us have paid dearly for free. Google gives away email that mines data and a search engine that has not improved since its inception and also mines data, and it above all gives away the feeling that there is no price for

2. Louis Menand, "A Critic at Large: Crooner in Rights Spat," *The New Yorker* (October 20, 2014), 84-6.

any of this. And if all of life could be contained by a Gmail account, that would work. If we were all computer geeks who never left our devices, Google could do it all. Luckily we are sentient still, and we love sensual pleasure still. We still want to have fun.

This is where Thomas Jefferson comes in: Those who believe that intellectual property rights ought to be more like a gift, and everything should just be real good for free, are drawn to our red-headed Founder. While, as one scholar notes, Jefferson's "aversion to property rights in ideas…happened to be extreme among the Framers rather than representative," Jefferson's 1813 letter to Isaac McPherson has been quoted by every advocate of the public domain since its discovery:

> It has been pretended by some, (and in England especially,) that inventors have a natural and exclusive right to their inventions, and not merely for their own lives, but inheritable to their heirs. But while it is a moot question whether the origin of any kind of property is derived from nature at all, it would be singular to admit a natural and even an hereditary right to inventors. It is agreed by those who have seriously considered the subject, that no individual has, of natural right, a separate property in an acre of land, for instance. By an universal law, indeed, whatever, whether fixed or movable, belongs to all men equally and in common, is the property for the moment of him who occupies it, but when he relinquishes the occupation, the property

goes with it. Stable ownership is the gift of social law, and is given late in the progress of society. It would be curious then, if an idea, the fugitive fermentation of an individual brain, could, of natural right, be claimed in exclusive and stable property. If nature has made any one thing less susceptible than all others of exclusive property, it is the action of the thinking power called an idea, which an individual may exclusively possess as long as he keeps it to himself; but the moment it is divulged, it forces itself into the possession of every one, and the receiver cannot dispossess himself of it. Its peculiar character, too, is that no one possesses the less, because every other possesses the whole of it. He who receives an idea from me, receives instruction himself without lessening mine; as he who lights his taper at mine, receives light without darkening me. That ideas should freely spread from one to another over the globe, for the moral and mutual instruction of man, and improvement of his condition, seems to have been peculiarly and benevolently designed by nature, when she made them, like fire, expansible over all space, without lessening their density in any point, and like the air in which we breathe, move, and have our physical being, incapable of confinement or exclusive appropriation. Inventions then cannot, in nature, be a subject of property. Society may give an exclusive right to the profits arising from them, as an encouragement to men to pursue ideas which may produce utility, but this may or may not be done, according to the will and convenience of the society, without claim or complaint from anybody. Accordingly, it is a fact, as far as I am informed, that England was, until we copied her, the only country on earth which ever, by a general law, gave a legal right to the exclusive use of an idea. In some other countries it is sometimes done, in a great case, and by a special and personal act, but, generally speaking, other nations have thought that these monopolies produce more embarrassment than advantage to society; and it may be observed that the nations which refuse monopolies of invention, are as fruitful as England in new and useful devices.

Considering the exclusive right to invention as given not of natural right, but for the benefit of society, I know well the difficulty of drawing a line between the things which are worth to the public the embarrassment of an exclusive patent, and those which are not. As a member of the patent board for several years, while the law authorized a board to grant or refuse patents, I saw with what slow progress a system of general rules could be matured...[3]

But this beautiful piece of correspondence doesn't say much, and contains factual errors: "[N]ations which refuse monopolies of invention" were not at all "as fruitful as England in new and useful devices." This was ridiculous: No other place was as advanced as England, the leader in the Industrial Revolution. Perhaps nations that had not yet joined modernity were not handing exclusive rights to inventors—but they were also likely lacking potable water and other necessities. Invention requires infrastructure. If

3. Jefferson, *The Writings of Thomas Jefferson*, vol. 20, 333-4.

human genius could thrive without a system to support it, Hollywood and Silicon Valley would be located in Papua New Guinea.

But they are not.

Rule of law matters, and getting it right matters, too. As creativity gets more and more particular, the legal regime needs to be more granular in its perfection to make it all work. The United States has created extraordinary things, mostly because it has been possible and wonderful and profitable to do so here in a way that isn't possible anywhere else in the world. To the extent that has broken down—and it has in the arts—the results are less good. They necessarily are: It takes the whole machine working smoothly to get to greatness, because greatness is rare and difficult.

That is the problem with Jefferson's fire metaphor: Neither fire nor ideas are stable. They change as they spread, and they change what they touch as they move along. Ideas become adulterated with other ideas the way fire becomes the thing that destroys furniture and houses and trees: Neither travels innocently, both transform and are transformed. At first it rings—or burns—true that "he who lights his taper at mine, receives light without darkening me." But a person casts a shadow, and he darkens the light you receive from a candle you share if he stands in the wrong place, tilts his head before the flame, waves his hand. Any presence changes the nature of the light, just as sharing an idea changes its form: It's not the same when you say it as it was in your mind. "Between thought and expression lies a lifetime," Lou Reed sang in 1968, with a long life still ahead. How many of us can articulate our thoughts as perfectly as they are when they hit like eureka? Expression is a miracle. Now try writing it down. Now try making it gorgeous. Now try making it perfect. An idea loses a lot and gains more as it hitchhikes its way through the world. But if it is expressed with the grace of a good cocktail at the end of a long and tiresome day, somebody did something right. That took work. That took some doing. That is something: *something*. It might even stabilize into something memorable and more than just an idea. There is art to that. As you might notice, littered and layered throughout this work are direct quotes, often at length, because to paraphrase would just not be the same. There are some perfect exact words.

And even at that, my selective citation has altered the original. Repetition of ideas wears them down and wears them out, gives them life and makes them brilliant, but it is transformative. Intellectual property is never rivalrous, because every time a book or movie or television show or song is interpreted—even by a person alone in his room enjoying it for its own sake—it is a new thing. A book is altered over time as it gains more readers, just as reactions change the nature of a visual entertainment: We live in an interactive world. The plot thickens and thins based on the ratings and viewer comments. That is why, per Marx, everything happens twice—first as tragedy then as comedy. That is why, per Gandhi, everything happens in four parts—they ignore you, they laugh at you, they fight you, you win. Art is in a feedback loop with its audience. Even the *Mona Lisa* is not the same now as it was in 1517 when King Francis I of France bought it for 4,000 écus after the death of Leonardo da Vinci. The *Mona Lisa* is the most famous painting ever: It is a permanent part of the Louvre, but the sale price if ever it were to happen would be ten figures. Perhaps you don't appreciate Francis Bacon's yellow triptych of Lucien Freud, but someone put $142 million worth of appreciation into it. The most beautiful painting is the one that fetched the highest price. Talent matters not at all if no one cares. Talent gets noticed.

And noticed a lot. All great experiences are tainted by other people's great experiences. In high school, I could read the exact same copy of *The Great Gatsby,* published by Charles Scribner's Sons in 1925, that my grandmother read while attending City College night school when it first came out, and we could both enjoy it equally: In that sense it's non-rivalrous. We cannot both eat the same Golden Delicious apple: In that sense it is rivalrous. But because time and history and movies have changed the meaning of both the book itself and of F. Scott Fitzgerald's life, we are having rival experiences: I have missed something and she has missed something—but the competition is metaphysical. We don't all get to have each other's lives. Lucky us.

Whoever invented the notion of non-rivalry lacked imagination and soul. How many times have I heard Bruce Springsteen's "Thunder Road"? I know it by heart, and not just the words, but the chord progressions, the drums that sound like we're pulling out of here to win. I know how the screen door slams and Mary's dress waves, and I can feel the breeze blowing. I know, and I am still so thrilled every time that song starts and I know pretty soon we'll be free and all the promises will be broken. I am jealous that somewhere right now this second this moment maybe in Malaysia, maybe in Liberia—but definitely in New Jersey—someone is hearing those words and that creaky harmonica for the first time and bubbles like a shaken-up Coca-Cola bottle are running through him because wow.

How lucky can you get that it is possible to be excited to death by three chords in three minutes, and it happens all the time? It happens with The Raspberries. It happens with Big Star. It happens with Cheap Trick. It happens with Vampire Weekend. I am told it happens with Justin Bieber. No one has the same experience of a stupid pop song as anyone else, and it is so nothing, but we would die without it. It is so not-nothing: It is sugar in the dullness of the day, and just as manna from heaven tasted like what you wanted it to, art is what it is to the beholder and not to anyone else. Within a single life of listening, a song does not remain the same. How I wish I could go back to the first time I heard The Doors play "Light My Fire," some glorious summer on WPLJ-FM in New York City when I was young and the opening organ sounded like nothing I'd ever heard before—instead of as it does now, like everything I've ever heard since. But I'll never get that back. No one can return to the first time. Gladly, I would never hear The Doors again. Gladly, everyone would never hear "Stairway to Heaven" again.

Then there are things that never stop sounding new, like Bob Dylan's voice. Pick any song, over and over again, singing Pushkin or pushpin, "Blowin' in the Wind" or blowing it completely, that voice always sounds new to me—as Saint Augustine said of God, its "beauty so ancient and so fresh." Bob Dylan's rasp was so worn-out always that it never wears on me: I'm sick of some of his albums, but I never tire of him. But that's a rare thing: a new and renewing experience within a single life. It is what Bruce Springsteen promises when he promises that all the promises will be broken: It is that which you cannot share, not even with yourself. It is the thing that makes you a virgin every time. Only art can do this, only genius calls this out of us. That is God revealing Himself.

It is not the same to hear *The Goldberg Variations* played by Johann Sebastian Bach himself as to hear the piece played by Glenn Gould either in the 1955 version or in his 1981 re-recording, one in 3/4 time, one in 4/4 time, the former known to be far superior to the latter. And, we can only guess that Bach himself was best of all, in his rustic clothes, in his German village church. Or not. And to add a twist, we might also guess that to see Gould perform live might have been, in the words of author Harold Brodkey, "to see Marxism die...Someone in actuality who had such a high immediate worth"[4]—though the pianist himself hated to play before an audience. Then you might make a case for the differences in quality between hearing Gould on compact disc or vinyl album, for fun you might throw in eight-track and cassette tapes as well, not to mention the many different brands and ranges of stereo equipment available to maximize the listening experience. As the 1993 movie *Thirty Two Short Films About Glenn Gould* aimed to show, there are so many renditions of the man himself, as many ways of seeing as there are audience members to see. As Heraclitus said, "No man steps into the same river twice." Of course not: Both man and river change, all the time.

The brilliance of the intellectual property system set up in this country is the way it is a gumball machine, it asks that you pay a dime before you blow your big pink bubble, that everyone puts in a little because each of us gets something from it. A public mural on a cement wall that brings pastels and brights to a haggard street and

4. Harold Brodkey, *Stories in an Almost Classical Mode* (Knopf, 1988), 163.

makes everyone stop and stare is obviously free, but look at all each of us gets from that moment of repose. We are so lucky to be an audience.

When Radiohead released *In Rainbows* in 2007 as an online download, they asked each listener to pay what he thought was the right amount, to choose his price. This was an experiment in idiosyncratic value, which means what it sounds like: Radiohead understood that *In Rainbows* might be worth one dollar to a nineteen-year-old coal miner in Beury, West Virginia, while it might be worth twenty dollars to a venture capitalist in Greenwich, Connecticut. The two cannot have the same experience of Radiohead when they have such different lives the rest of the time, one almost never seeing the light, the other hardly ever seeing the darkness (you decide which is which). Of course, because this happened on the Internet, most people did what they could do: They swiped *In Rainbows* for free.[5]

Otherwise, just as time wounds all heels, time is the avenger in its effects on every idea, every piece of work put out there. Occasionally, it ages some thing of beauty gracefully, but mostly ideas are indeed rivalrous, for they wear out like shoes as they walk along. The guy with the really great stock tip first is in a different position than the

5. http://musically.com/2008/10/15/exclusive-warner-chappell-reveals-radioheads-in-rainbows-pot-of-gold/.

27th man to hear it, or the 270th man to hear it, and far better off than the 27,000th man to hear it. Which is why Bill Gates has more money than any of us: He was in on Microsoft first. And that's why America has more money than God: The country made a decision early on to reward people with good ideas in property incentives, and that turned out to be a very good generator of progress—the one with the best idea first makes more money than the one who thought of it 27th or 27,000th and so on.

In Thomas Jefferson's letter to Isaac McPherson, he sets intellectual property ablaze, and he also sets the proposition of private property itself on fire. But his was an intellectual game, because Thomas Jefferson was not willing to burn the deed to Monticello, or to free his slaves.

11

As a writer, I wish copyright never ended, that it were like a house—really a home—or some other heirloom I could pass on for generations, fee simple. "A man builds a house. With his own hands, let us say, in order to keep the analogy simple," wrote Authors' League president Gertrude Atherton in *The New York Times* in 1917. "He sells that house....It is precisely the same with an author. We build a book in our brains. We sell it to the public through our agent, the publisher. The money received is capital. In the old days the book was bought outright. Today he is more in the position of an auctioneer. He may venture a sum in advance royalties, but for the rest he does the best he can to make the public play and buy the wares with which the maker entrusts him."[1] Before I had studied intellectual property law, I assumed that somewhere out

1. Gertrude Atherton, "The Tax on Authors' Earnings," *The New York Times,* June 25, 1917.

there, Jason Twain was collecting the proceeds on *Huckle-berry Finn,* that Jennifer Bunyan was reaping the rewards of *The Pilgrim's Progress.*

Of course, few family homes—even if they are mansions and especially if they are McMansions—last for generations. Just because Buckingham Palace has been with the Windsors for centuries does not make the rest of us like royalty. Mostly we will be lucky to own a floor-through in gentrifying Bed-Stuy until we are ready for assisted living, and so it has ever been. Nothing lasts, and worse still, nothing lasts for long: Eighty-seven percent of the companies in the Fortune 500 in 1955 were no longer on that list in 2011;[2] a full third of the Fortune 500 from 1970 was gone by 1983.[3] As individuals, we don't do much better: Two-thirds of the time a private fortune does not outlive its heirs, and it only makes it past the third generation ten percent of the time.[4] The world moves quickly and a lot happens—and nothing lasts. There is hardly a chance that a book will still be selling when its copyright expires seventy years after the author's death.

And then there is Shakespeare.

As Samuel Johnson remarked in 1773, "There seems

2. http://csinvesting.org/2012/01/06/fortune-500-extinction/.

3. http://www.businessweek.com/chapter/degeus.htm.

4. http://finance.yahoo.com/news/want-wealth-last-generations-check-130000670.html.

to be...in authours a stronger right of property than that by occupancy; a metaphysical right, a right, as it were, of creation, which should from its nature be perpetual....["][5] And back in the nineteenth century, the poet Robert Southey—and even then poets were not in it for the money—was bold enough to ask, "[U]pon what principle, with what justice, or under what pretext of public good, are men of letters deprived of a perpetual property in the produce of their own labours, when all other persons enjoy it as their indefeasible right—a right beyond the power of any earthly authority to take away? Is it because their labour is so light—the endowments which it requires so common—the attainments so cheaply and easily acquired, and the present remuneration so adequate, so ample, and so certain?"[6] Writing is the most difficult thing you can do sitting down—and it is much harder to do in any other position. Even writing badly is not easy. To come up with *the quality of mercy is not strained* is to labor for the ages. It never occurred to me that such imprints as Signet Classics were benefiting greatly because *Romeo and Juliet* had passed into the public domain, that those lovely editions of, yes, *Aereopagitica* from Everyman's Library

5. Mark Rose, *Authors and Owners: The Invention of Copyright* (Harvard University Press, 1993), 85.

6. Mark Rose, "Nine-tenths of the Law: The English Copyright Debates and the Rhetoric of the Public Domain," 75, 82.

were so inexpensive because the text cost nothing—and there is no known Nigel Shakespeare or Georgina Milton collecting royalty checks, while Random House prospers. In fact, as Mark Rose points out, "Milton's descendants...died in poverty and...Shakespeare's descendants [lived] in poverty."[7]

Of course, that's the way the fortune cookie crumbles. Money does not last past two generations. Copyright is not to blame.

And copyright is designed to create continual struggle. We do our best work when we are striving. If it's too easy, nothing happens. J. D. Salinger lived most of his life—modestly, in New Hampshire, but with kids and nannies and affairs—off the proceeds of one novel. Imagine all the writing he might have done if forced. Surely there was more to Salinger than *The Catcher in the Rye* and several short stories perfectly arrayed to delight *New Yorker* readers. Creative people need to prove they are exceptional, and once they have done that, sometimes they are done. But even if they keep going, so often the most amazing offerings are the early stuff. The extraordinary loveliness of what is produced by an artist when he is young and trying to make a name—there is still no better Philip Roth than *Goodbye, Columbus* and no finer Jay McInerney than *Bright Lights, Big City*. We all get better and sharper and

7. *Ibid.*

smarter with age, but we are never so keen and alive as when we are screaming to be heard.

Copyright is designed to keep the process going. It is meant to pay the rent and keep the work moving along. Ideally, we are always screaming to be heard one more time. Consider this: We tend to think of Hollywood the way immigrants envision America—as a place where the streets are paved in gold. And while movie stars might continue to trip the life fantastic, and indeed there are plenty of Bentleys lining the parking lanes of Rodeo Drive, a November 2007 report—that has anecdotally been widely accredited by those in show business—informs that: "Making movies—as distinct from owning libraries of fully-amortized films that continue to throw off sizable profits—has gone from a modestly profitable activity to one that now generates…substantial losses over the initial release of films to all worldwide markets, a period of roughly five years."[8] Even if a film enters an era of black ink five years after its release, a company needs a large backlog of movies that have made money and continue to make money to finance its ongoing operations, which in effect pays for the creativity of lots of individual people, from crappy crapshoot to genuine genius. The more there is, the more there is.

8. http://www.screendigest.com/press/releases/FHAN-78WF4M/pressRe-
    lease.pdf.

Perhaps the threat of poverty has pushed people along in a way that it just doesn't in, say, France, which produces some of the shittiest rock music known to mankind. Perhaps life is so easy in Norway, which as a country possesses so much oil that the entire population could apparently sleep for twenty years with minimal economic consequences, that it has failed to deliver much in the way of innovation to the world. Nonetheless, French fashion is still the sine qua non, and Ingmar Bergman is still the filmmaker's filmmaker: Art happens. It is hard to say that the people producing this work have made a wise choice, if satisfaction is any measure. According to one study published in 2006 by the Economic and Social Research Council, some of the happiest people in the world—though possibly not the most inventive—are in Bangladesh, where the typical income is a dollar a day. And yet according to the ESRC report, "artisans are the unhappiest among all the occupational groups, with 40 percent claiming to be 'not too happy' and only 8.3 percent 'very happy.'"[9]

Is creativity helped or hindered by a life of luxury? The answer elusively eludes us because there are so many examples and counterfactuals to prove either side of the

---

9. L. Camfield, K. Choudhury, and J. Devine, "Relationships, Happiness and Well-Being: Insights From Bangladesh," (Economic and Social Research Council, 2006), 10. http://www.welldev.org.uk/research/workingpaperpdf/wed14.pdf.

argument, the story of the brilliant scholar who achieved tenure and turned out no further discoveries, matched by the tale of Vincent van Gogh, who despite a life of hardship gave us his beautiful haystacks, and then some. We can only look at averages: and on average, most of what is averagely good and useful and enjoyable that was made in America was made by the middle class. Or the workingman or the wealthy woman, but roughly what we call middle-class people. Writers and painters and filmmakers are incentivized by money, just like everyone else, and the need to make a living is the best reason to get out of bed and do great work. The story of art in America, of science in the States, is the story of people from solid homes doing good work in safely pleasant circumstances, with just a little bit of that edge, that challenge, mostly of people telling them it can't be done, that gives anyone with a dream the necessary determination.

For a long time it worked out very well. It has always been difficult to be a successful creative person, because talent is rare, but the rewards were good. They had to be. Consider how boring most people are. Consider how often you sit and talk to someone and wish you could leave, because he is not interesting at all. Then think about a book you can't put down and hope will never end: The author is not even in the room and is only holding your attention with words on a page, but he has you trapped and you don't want to ever escape. Most people, using everything they have in real life, cannot take hold of you the way a talented writer can without even being there. Talent is the ability to mesmerize people when you are nowhere near. Talent is the ability to make something that is more stunning than human presence.

There are many factors that drive creativity, but one of them is not patent or copyright law. Yes, the existence of these things to begin with, the fact that money can be made from what you make, matters a lot. But the particulars of the law drive only one kind of creativity: that of legal scholars, who generate a great deal of copy arguing about the rights and wrongs of the system. Which is what they are meant to do: That's their creativity. Some of it is extremely inventive, and entertaining. Copyright infringement did not even prevent the creation of *The Grey Album*, a genuinely original musical montage by Danger Mouse, which blended together The Beatles' *White Album* with Jay-Z's *Black Album*. This mashup combined a cappella versions of the rapper's work—which had been released with Jay-Z's implicit permission to be used for sampling and remixing purposes—with instrumentals from the Fab Four's classic masterpiece. It was positively reviewed in *The New Yorker* and chosen as the best album of 2004 by *Entertainment Weekly*; the collective critical community ranked it tenth in *The Village Voice* Pazz & Jop poll for that year. *The Grey Album* was released to limited outlets and only sold 3,000 copies, but since Danger Mouse never got permission to use The Beatles' material, record label EMI instantly took action to block its further distribution. All this led to Grey Tuesday, an electronic act of civil disobedience, in which 170 individual websites allowed users to download *The Grey Album* for free for 24 hours; over 100,000 copies of the album were burned from the Web that gray day. And the legal repercussions were minimal: EMI sent cease-and-desist letters around, but life went on.

My guess is that Paul and Ringo, along with the administrators of the estates of John and George, would have given Danger Mouse permission to do what he did. Or not. Or possibly for a sum. I mean, we all know The Beatles can afford to be generous. And some of the best hip-hop songs are based on previous recordings, sampled generously, with tolls paid: A Tribe Called Quest's "Can I Kick It?" draws on Lou Reed's opening riff in "Walk on the Wild Side"; De La Soul's "Eye Know" relies completely on Steely Dan's "Peg"; and Public Enemy's "He Got Game" includes the guitar lead and chorus from Buffalo Springfield's "For What It's Worth." But given that Danger Mouse used such substantial sections of The Beatles' work wholesale, it amounts to stealing—even if he threw a great party with the swag. At any rate, he did do it regardless, he expressed himself completely and then faced the legal ramifications later on, once his opus was out there to receive response. Copyright law did not shut off his creativity: It gave the project notoriety. It created something more: controversy. And hullabaloo has been the heart of rock 'n' roll since the day they started censoring the shake, rattle, and roll of Elvis' hips. I'm not saying that the lawyers and their letters are not an obnoxious pain in the ass; I'm just saying this is all part of the game. The kids posting their wild animés on YouTube, mixing Mickey Mouse with Danger Mouse, pitting Marilyn Manson against Marilyn Monroe, sampling this and tasting that, cutting collage and mixing montage and electronic decoupage, are not blocked from their brilliance. Sometimes they fight the law; sometimes the law wins.

According to the Bureau of Labor Statistics, the median annual income for salaried writers was $55,940 in May 2012,[10] which is not so bad. But this number encompasses the earnings of authors, screenwriters, admen, and even lyricists. We tend to believe that the Internet has destroyed the printed page and made it harder for writers to make money, but back in 1995, before blogs, here is what a survey from the National Writers' Union reported:

> Writers' incomes fall well below those of comparably educated Americans. The average income for individuals who hold bachelor's degrees is $29,868. Yet while 91 percent

10. http://www.bls.gov/ooh/media-and-communication/writers-and-authors.htm.

of surveyed writers hold B.A.s and 50 percent, graduate degrees, their income is significantly lower. Looking at writing income during 1991-1993, a typical writer with 15 years experience earned a median annual income of $4,000 from freelancing. Staff jobs brought in $25,000. Long term contracts – held by writers who are not employees but have ongoing agreements with publishers – earned $12,500. While writers tend to write in several genres, a majority – 68 percent – earn income in only one employee relationship – either freelance, staff, or contract.

The number of writers who earn middle class incomes is surprisingly low. While 61 percent work full time at their writing craft, only 16 percent of freelance writers earn $30,000 or more. Some 39 percent of staff writers and 24 percent of contract writers do.

Nonwriting income – earned by 53 percent – averaged $17,500. Sources of this income included self employment, reported by 21 percent; salaries, 18 percent; hourly wages, 11 percent; and government subsidies, 3 percent. Investment income was reported by 23 percent – indicating 77 percent have no substantial savings. In addition, 33 percent stated they had neither pension nor retirement funds set aside.

Writers' households, with an average of 2.2 residents, recorded a median income of $40,000.[11]

11. Nancy DuVergne Smith, "The Freelance Writers' Lot: The NWU American Writers Survey Profiles" (National Writers Union, 1995). http://members.aol.com/nancyds/ wlot1.html.

Plainly, there are too many writers. Or there are too many people trying to be writers. There are too many people trying to be all kinds of things that are difficult. This has always been true, and were it not we would have no waiters and no bartenders. The world is full of people who would like to do things they can't. But before everyone had an eight-megapixel camera on his iPhone, it was a lot more difficult for amateurs to imagine they could compete with Richard Avedon. Technology has made it possible to be expressive for fun in more ways. Copyright has always been the best filter for talent, because if it was good, you knew it because you got paid. That is the best formula. Anything else is noise.

12

This is a lament for a way of life that is lost, and for all that will no longer be. But should it be? "If I had asked people what they wanted, they would have said faster horses," said Henry Ford, which is a reminder that we quarrel with progress at our peril. And it is progress: Progress is painful. No doubt people had a hard time adjusting to the intrusions of the telephone call in 1876, and surely they hated the way the day lasted well into the night once electricity came along in 1879. Imagine the horror of having to be hygienic and smell fresh and clean at even the lesser occasions when bathing with soap indoors became a fin-de-siècle phenomenon. The Internet could hardly be harder to cope with than a bubble bath. So what if the Great American Novel is a relic, if the Hollywood blockbuster is a thing of the past, if the seventy-minute concept album is no more? If they all die of lack of demand, so what? People have not stopped reading or watching or listening—they just do it another way. Contra

King Solomon, there is always something new under the sun, even if it's the same old thing. Perhaps the nature of expression has changed, but human nature has not. What goes around goes around—literally, but differently: We used to spin 45s on our turntables, now we listen to downloads from iTunes. The hit single is back. It is 1959 all over again. From transistor radio to iPhone in half a century. The Beatles made us switch to long-playing records, to full-length albums, but that was a long time ago. Here we are now: hello.

I don't blame the Internet for ruining everything. I blame stupidity. They published books people would never read. They released albums no one could stand to listen to—or worse, no one was interested enough in to not stand. They made movies that put the audience to sleep. The standard should have been all books that are in stores are impossible to put down, all movies are in some sense thrillers, and all albums we send out to the world make everyone want to get on their feet and dance or protest or do something—something like cry until they slit their wrists. If art is not a crime spree, what is the point? But that is not what was going on. It was not. Back before there was an Internet to blame for the destruction of an assortment of businesses that cater to people's desire to be entertained and enlightened, these companies were very badly run, because money was plentiful and they could be.

So they indulged weird idiosyncrasies, and not just

occasionally, forgetting that is what Scotland and Bolivia are for. They bored people, with world music and with experimental fiction, when you do not even let Bob Woodward be boring, because what is worse? But they did that. And not just occasionally at all. They did it all the time, because they could afford to and it was someone's taste and he insisted at the meeting until everyone else was spent with arguing. For the two hundred and thirty-one mistakes they did not make, they made seven hundred and sixty-eight more. They signed every band that sounded at all like the Eagles or even looked it, then they let them make four albums that all failed in studios in LA, with session musicians and tour support and on and on, because they still had second homes in Malibu and then some after the losses—and because the Eagles sound like cocaine going up someone's nose. They gave first-time novelists half-a-million-dollar deals for hype's sake. They made long, boring epic movies for tens of millions of dollars—so many of them—and let accountants sort it all out. They had no business plan. Actually, their plan was America and hegemony. No one told them hope is not a plan. No one warned them that nerds who never had any fun anyway and could not dance and did not feel would come along and ruin everything.

No one told them that nothing lasts.

Now look. *Look*: There is a great library of American film and literature and music that will always exist, but the infrastructure to make more of it is thoroughly degraded. We still create, but we do it a lot less, and less successfully. Everything has changed.

Deep Throat was right when he told Woodward and Bernstein to follow the money, because activity goes where it is rewarded. Willie Sutton robbed banks, because that's where the money is. Money explains everything. Used to be, if you were a hard-luck kid in a dead-end town in a flyover state, you learned to play the guitar—or the bass, or drums if you were hyperactive—because maybe you could join a band and hit the road and make it big. And even if that did not work, at least along the way you could get laid. At least along the way, you could get out of town. At least along the way, something instead of nothing.

Now every kid wants to invent the next big app. That's the way out: Coming up with something clever that consumers will die without on their mobile devices. This is, of course, the opposite of cool. What is more nerdy than tinkering with technology that is not even likely to be fun?

But the last real rock star was Axl Rose, and the last reluctant rock star was Kurt Cobain, so what is the point of amping up in the garage? Even kids know this. Even kids who are not yet wise to paying bills follow the money. Money is more than just rent and emeralds, money is more than just meals and platinum, money is more than the many things it buys and funds and pays for: Money is glitter. Money is attention. Money is where the action is. If something is valuable, it generates excitement. What is worthless gets lost, and lost to history. Now that there is no money in being a musician because no one buys albums anymore, the dream is no longer to be on stage beneath the bright strobe spotlight at Madison Square Garden. The dream is a tech startup.

The dream is a life of headaches.

Music still exists. It is still made and sold. But no one loves it the way teenagers used to love it. That is not possible, because the message is the medium, and downloads don't feel like LPs. They don't feel like anything at all. Rock 'n' roll saved my life, because I would gather my allowance and my babysitting money and buy a record and listen to it over and over and over again obsessively and completely. I listened to the bad songs. I replayed the good songs. I stood up and moved the needle or rewound the tape to hear a song I loved again and again and again. I got very attached to the music I bought. It meant a lot to me. I listened alone, and I made other people listen. And I listened alone some more. This is how I became a fanatical lover of words and melody. And there is no other way it happens. You can't get insane over a band or a singer-songwriter because one song you bought on iTunes made you smile or teared you up. Fanaticism is a commitment, and teenagers were way in deep for many decades, because buying prerecorded music on vinyl or tape or CD pulled them in. That hardly exists anymore, and the kind of love that went with it is gone. It has to be.

Love is a rare and special thing, and it happens only because the circumstances are perfect. Love requires serious moonlight. No one loves music unless they own it and hold it and look at it and live with it and listen to it all the time because it is the biggest thing in life.

Music can't be the biggest thing in life anymore because it isn't.

The teenager is gone. As a group, teenagers came and went with the twentieth century. They were born with the invention of leisure and the end of child labor—and the beginning of the yelping teenyboppers at Frank Sinatra concerts. Starting in the 1950s, adolescence became a liminal state between childhood and responsibility, when rebellion in ways that annoyed your parents but were otherwise harmless became available. Does that exist anymore? People of all ages smoke marijuana and listen to Mumford & Sons, while high school students do their homework and worry about the future. Everyone in every demographic is on Facebook all the time when they should be doing something else. There hardly seems a special culture that is just youthful, except perhaps for vampire movies. When I think about being fifteen without The Clash, I shudder. But that was a different world.

I wonder what kids do with their anxiety instead. Social media only makes it more extreme. You look at your phone for a while and get caught up until you get bored and put it down. You look at your laptop for a while until you get tired and stop. Then you do it again. The Internet is more like all that we are trying to escape: It magnifies crazy. And yet this is what we do now with our downtime—and our uptime. Music is a grandiose way out, getting caught up in rock star personalities and fixating on lyrics are all part of it, and that exit is gone.

We are here to be entertained. We are not here to do a Google search. We are not here to stare into the void. We are here to have fun.

13

___

What is the nature of American creativity? Did the Constitution create America?

Of course it did. By subjecting creativity to a market system from the get-go, the Constitution made this the most commercially inventive and artistic country ever. We make beautiful things and great stuff that sells, and what does not sell disappears to somewhere else, to somewhere beyond eighty percent off. The term "intellectual property" was coined in an 1845 Massachusetts Circuit Court opinion, in which Judge Charles L. Woodbury noted that "the labors of the mind, productions and interests [are] as much a man's own…as the wheat he cultivates, or the flocks he rears."[1] But creators' rights were never the point—they were simply an incentive. The Founders, after

___

1. Charles Levi Woodbury and George Minot, *Reports of Cases Argued and Determined in the Circuit Court of the United States for the First Circuit*, vol. I (Charles C. Little and James Brown, 1847), 57.

all, says legal historian Alexander Lindey, "entertained a low opinion of all estate, which they regarded as transient property."[2] But they did believe in popular rule, and the arts—both fine and useful—had to earn their own keep, which meant that what did not widely appeal did not stand a chance. When you consider the extent to which culture is devalued in the United States unless it is profitable, bear in mind this is just our way, and so it has ever been. If you have come to America to starve, why have you come at all? Here we don't dream of being an artist or a guitarist—in America everyone wants to be a rock star.

When the Founding Fathers thought of patent and copyright, their immediate desires might have been relatively modest. They wanted the grammar books of their good friend Noah Webster published in the United States, they needed legal texts for their own purposes, and they hoped the classics they so enjoyed would be more readily available domestically. They wished to join the Industrial Revolution. And yes, they desired a public sphere, an educated citizenry, and a reading class of people who could be trusted to conduct themselves in a democracy. At the time they surely could not have conceived of Hollywood movies and Silicon Valley software, they could not have imagined iPods and iPhones and iPads leading to e-commerce and e-trade on trains and planes and automobiles.

2. Alexander Lindey, *Plagiarism and Originality* (Harper & Brothers, 1952), 96.

But in twenty-first century America, we cannot suffer a life without these luxuries that have become necessities. It wasn't until the twentieth century that the United States came into its own as a center of culture, and this might be the result of a lack of government support for such ventures. Or perhaps it is youth. We were a net importer of art and literature until World War I, and even our magnificent military was the eighteenth largest on earth—nestled between Portugal's and Bulgaria's in rank—when World War II began, before the nation mobilized like crazy. It takes time to make something of yourself. It just does.

This country was founded on suspicion—of government, of royalty, of entrenched interests—so it had to develop with minimal interference from on high. As such, patents to encourage manufacturing are not merely good because they save the state money—they are also good because they leave it out of the decision altogether. "The refined view," explains University of Texas law professor Oren Bracha, "not only recognized the cost advantage associated with patents, but also saw as an advantage the fact that government did not employ discrimination or discretion by evaluating the utility or desirability of particular inventions, whose value was left to the market."[3]

3. Oren Bracha, "The Commodification of Patents 1600-1836: How Patents Became Rights and Why We Should Care," *Loyola of Los Angeles Law Review* 38 (2004): 177, 208.

Similarly, there was no state apparatus that pushed along the great copyright and trademark fields, our big movies are not underwritten by the government as they are in so many European countries, the glorious fashions of Calvin Klein and Marc Jacobs are not made in nationalized assembly lines, deregulation is the rule in all industry. Bicycle designers Wilbur and Orville Wright flew their first glider on the beach in Kitty Hawk, not at a United States Air Force base. We don't just distrust government to run things—we also assume it has terrible taste and can't fly.

———

The greatest of the great American art forms have been done in factory settings, with profit in mind. While we have produced some of the best and best-known fine artists in the world—Willem de Kooning, Jackson Pollock, Jennifer Bartlett, Andrew Wyeth, Mark Rothko, Robert Rauschenberg, Helen Frankenthaler—and the some of the most revered literaticians—Norman Mailer, Philip Roth, Toni Morrison, Cormac McCarthy, Joan Didion, Ernest Hemingway—the world clamors for our movies and our music most of all. And these are produced in group process, in assembly-line fashion, with commercial intent. This is what we are better at doing than anyone else on

Earth. This is not to say that the films of Antonioni and Fellini are not as great as an awful lot of what we make here—but Italian-American directors like Scorsese and Coppola have done far more with the art form than the forbearers they left behind. Sure, the French create great cinema, but Americans make magnificent movies.

Consider the nominees for the Academy Award for Best Picture in 1997: *Titanic, As Good As It Gets, L.A. Confidential, Good Will Hunting,* and *The Full Monty.* My vote would have been for *Good Will Hunting,* because it was a fun and funny script, it was a love story with a happy ending, it was about a math genius struggling to be less so, it was set at my alma mater, and it presented a psychiatrist who still had not recovered from a Bostonian's PTSD after Bill Buckner's last-minute mishap in the 1986 World Series. But I understand why *Titanic,* despite its sloppy screenplay, had to win: Of all those movies, it is the only one that was necessarily made in America. It is the white t-shirt with the label inside that somehow, even at this late hour, is marked in all caps: MADE IN AMERICA. *Titanic* cost millions upon millions of dollars—and that is just the budget overages. It had grandiose special effects, it had class conflict on the high seas, it had a very bad pop song by a big-voiced singer that was absolutely unbearable and stuck in your brain like damage, it had movie stars with movie-star looks, it had jewels and treasure, it was gushy and romantic, it was based on a truly colossal true story of a true shipwreck, it was a remake of *A Night To Remember* which never should have been made in the first place, it had a director with a temper, it had trouble on the set, it was itself nearly the Hollywood equivalent of the story it told, yet it became one of the great box-office successes of all time. We give Oscars for quality, and *Titanic* had quality: It had American quality. It was massive. It was intense and ridiculous and had so many opportunities to fail, and yet somehow—*voilà!*—when Leo drowned in the Atlantic, we all cried. *Titanic* has perfect pitch for every heroic myth. It is large and contains multitudes. Big is beautiful. And *Titanic* is the size of Hollywood.

No one can convince me that Hollywood is not the greatest artist ever. I cannot imagine who or what even comes close. Take that, Michelangelo.

I am halfway through life, and I have not yet been within the pristine walls of the Sistine Chapel, but I would die without movies. What would I do without *Apocalypse Now*? Where would I be without *Annie Hall*? How would I know what it all means without *Blade Runner*? Based on a prescient piece of speculative fiction by Philip K. Dick, *Blade Runner* is Ridley Scott's 1982 masterwork about a human being who hunts down fake human beings who are such precise replications of the real thing that they are called "replicants." Because Dick specialized in the paranoid style of chasing one's own tale, the replicant-hunter may be a replicant himself. Probably. Aren't we all? How do we know this is not just a dream after all? *Blade Runner* is a great movie about authenticity, because the fake human beings are even better at being human than the real ones, right down to the flaws. So what's so great about authenticity? Love is an illusion, conjured from what we choose to believe about another person. Does it matter if that person is real or like real? Does it matter if our emotions are real or like real? Is there a difference? "We are what we pretend to be," wrote Kurt Vonnegut in *Mother Night* in 1961, "so we must be careful about what we pretend to be." The movies are pretend, which is why they are what we are. That big overwhelming screen and surround sound sink into our conscious and unconscious deeper than dreams. We walk around in a state of narrative. Life is more like a movie than it is like life.

And some of the finest films, in the cineaste sense, were made in Hollywood when the studio system was in place, and directors were simply cranking out product. Screenwriters were crammed into bungalow offices, churning scripts for directors under contract and actors groomed for stardom. And yet, of the many movies that John Ford made because he had to, because he was paid to, probably ten or twenty of them are great art, classics, as good as it gets. Because when you take a genius and put him in any setting, including one that is the artistic equivalent of a factory, art will come out. Artists make art. John Ford couldn't help it. He was a great filmmaker, working with talented people, and he made great films. It is for this same reason that those songs written by teams in rows of rooms in the Brill Building or in cubicles in the Motown studios are as emotionally resonant and haunting as the dark part of the night when the sky is big and there are no stars, no moon, and all is terrifying. Talented people do not need atmosphere to work. They do not need inspiration. They just need time and payment. They need to treat what they do like a job. They need to show up. Writing the Great American Novel has more in common with coal mining than it does with keeping a journal—it is hard labor, long and intense. You cannot learn to be talented—you are born that way. After that, it is all a matter of behaving like everybody else and doing the work. This is what Americans understand very well. We do not romanticize creativity. "Business should adapt to art and not the other way around," says the eponymous soprano in Jean-Jacques Beineix's 1981 cult classic *Diva*—which is surely what they believe in France. In the United States, you know you are talented because somebody is paying for your work.

Even Andy Warhol, who was after all a painter, had his Factory. No one knows how much painting Warhol did himself, if at all. And I mean, *if at all*: Warhol believed in delegating; he was the Ronald Reagan of painters. Do you doubt that he is a genius? He invented a world. In fact, his genius was in the concept, the recapitulative, regurgitative repetition of tomato soup cans, of Marilyn Monroe's silk-screened face, of car accident photographs—of art in ideas. Coming from an industrial town like Pittsburgh, with a background in window-dressing for fashion boutiques and department stores, Warhol's all-American instinct was to make art into a commercial process and popularize it, to make Pop Art. No other painter before or since Warhol—whose works hang all over the world—also has the distinction of producing one of the most important rock albums ever made: the debut of the Velvet Underground, whose cover is graced by a bright yellow banana he painted (or someone did). While *The Velvet Underground and Nico* hardly sold at all when it was released in 1965, it is one of the most significant contributions to music, #13 on *Rolling Stone*'s list of the five hundred best albums ever. In 2006, it was added to the National Recording Registry by the Library of Congress, where it hangs out with *Born to Run* by Bruce Springsteen, *Pet Sounds* by the Beach Boys, *Time Out* by the Dave Brubeck Quartet, and the "I Have a Dream" speech. There is no guitar band that comes along anywhere in the Western Hemisphere that is not a Velvet Underground rip-off. Right now, in a basement on the outskirts of Prague, someone is learning to play "I'm Waiting for the Man" on a third-hand Fender with replacement parts. And no painter has replaced Warhol: Both his name and his images are more famous than any others. Of course they are: Who does not know Campbell's and Brillo? We live in the culture that Warhol manufactured. He is forever now.

Warhol is one of these men who proves a great thing: Creativity happens. It happens with soup cans and soupçons, choose your form. In a land as vast and noisy as the United States, one that is both very rich and very desperate, expressiveness is both many splendored and undervalued, and what is good emerges and what is lousy has its moment and passes. Or all is lost, too much is found. You might think that 2 Live Crew and Motley Crüe and Freddy Krueger are utter crap, but they are both the lowest common denominator and the highest median of their kind—and not everyone enjoys Glenn Gould, who is, at any rate, Canadian. And still, in all the noise, people will discover a little movie like *The Artist* and make it a big hit, audiences continue to gather around the things they continue together around: Discovery happens. It is still possible to be surprised and awed by the great out there.

But of course it's not the same. Hegemony is over. The days where everybody rushed out to Sam Goody to buy the new Beatles album as soon as it came out, the days when lines formed around the block at New York's Ziegfeld Theater because the latest installment of *Star Wars* had opened—the days when certain cultural moments captured everybody together as if we'd all been granted a brief furlough from the prisonhouse of reality—live on only in mild forms, in those crazy Harry Potter fans, in those of us who will still preorder a Springsteen album from Amazon.com. And still this is not a country that values the small gesture, the way they do in Holland or Belgium, and yet we are becoming a nation of microcommunities with microtrends, the world is getting larger and each individual is becoming lesser. There is far more excitement at the introduction of a new Apple device—pre-dawn lines for iPads—or in the life-altering app than there is when anything artistic happens, because there's so much, too much, it's all coming at us through every available conduit.

We download life.

The creative form hardly affected at all by the encroachments of technology—at least insofar as its market has not caved—is the fine arts, like painting and sculpture. I imagine an art dealer working in New York or London or Shanghai today would not find it difficult to adjust to the conditions of Paris or Rome during the Renaissance. Obviously, the currencies and the names have changed—at least mostly—but add a few or many zeroes, and it is the same business of discovering talent and pleasing patrons and flattering egos on all sides of the bargain. You still cannot download a painting, it is still possessed of the thingness of the thing it is, there is still no substitute for brushstrokes on the surface. A work of art is valued as an object, and somehow world wars and nuclear bombs and collapsing towers have not destroyed our ability to prize what is decorative and invested with meaning and intensity and talent. People with loads of money buy great art quite ravenously, and maybe it is just a commodity, but they could put all their doremi in a copper mine, and they don't. Talent is devastating, even to the very rich, even to those beyond contempt, which is why the cost of a piece by Richard Prince or Brice Marden is still exorbitant. At a Christie's auction on November 12, 2013, Jeff Koons' ten-foot stainless steel *Balloon Dog (Orange)* fetched a price of $58.4 million, above the $55 million estimate, setting a record for the most ever paid for the work of a living artist. This was also a serious leap over the previous record, which had been set in May 2013 when Gerhard Richter's painting *Domplatz, Mailand* sold for $37.1 million at Sotheby's. Of course, when the Francis Bacon triptych went for $142.4 million, this all became old news. And it became older news when the New York auctions of contemporary art in May 2014 racked up $1.6 billion in sales. This was after a lovely self-portrait by Andy Warhol commanded $30 million at Art Basel. But perhaps the art market is finding its level: These numbers are not so different from the extraordinary highs before the financial crash, when Sotheby's and Christie's reported a return of $1.7 billion for November 2007 alone, up twenty-four

percent from the previous year. An AIDS charity art auction at Sotheby's, organized by Bono on Valentine's Day
2008, netted sales of $42.6 million for just one
night—coming out well ahead of the expected $29 mil-
lion.[4]

It is an extraordinary thing to sell a painting at all.
That must be nice. So it must be the craziest humdinger
ever to be Jeff Koons and get crazy money for these enor-
mous metal toys he builds that are inexplicable and out-
rageous. But do you know who is not at all surprised? Do
you know who was expecting this all along? Jeff Koons. I
am sure of it. I am not saying this because I know anything at all about him, but the work tells me everything.
And he could not make a big bright heart the size of a
Mack truck—bigger—and call it art even though he surely
knows how to sketch faces and bodies anatomically perfectly unless he were sure he is a genius. And because he
knows, the rest of us know it, too. You may not like Jeff
Koons, and you may not understand why anything he does
is so great, but it is. It has soul and guts, and he is very
loud. The noise, the colorful noise, must sound like money
to the billionaires who buy Koons. The art market is a

4. Jennifer S. Lee, "A (Red) Auction at Sotheby's, to Raise the Stakes," *The New
York Times* (February 15, 2008). http://cityroom.blogs.nytimes.com/2008/
02/15/the-red-campaign-comes-to-sothe-
bys/?_php=true&_type=blogs&_r=0.

blooming tulip bubble and Jeff Koons is the most fecund bulb of all.

Not that I know anything at all about art, but I know a lot about talent. Talent is not just one thing, it is a valise of hellfire. Talent is being extraordinary at a particular thing, but it also being extraordinary at everything else: It is having a huge personality that will not quit, it is tirelessness when other people are exhausted and done, it is screaming at people to listen when they don't want to and somehow convincing them they will die if they don't, it is being sure you are talented even when you are not sure, it is doing the same thing over and over and over and over again and then some until it is perfect and still not being satisfied, it is never being satisfied, it is being indifferent to other people's talent, it is being indifferent to other people's anything at all, it is hard work every day, it is more screaming at people, it is charm, it is a complete commitment to nothing but the thing you are talented at. Talent is a world. If you have a normal life, you are not talented, because that is not possible. Jeff Koons is talented. Obviously.

It turns out that creativity that relies on the goodness of wealthy patrons, like fine art, which was not all that much affected by the coming of copyright, will finally fare better in a world in which technology reduces much of invention to cleverness, and much of cleverness to piracy. But this is antithetical to the American mission. Nothing against all the great fine artists this country has produced, but they are a carryover from Europe; they are Old World. We'll never conquer the planet with brushes and clay and pencils the way we did with celluloid and vinyl and acetate. If our most original painter was Pollock, he was still no Picasso, and we all know it, which is why Matthew Barney and Julian Schnabel and David Salle all started directing films. Our movies are America. And the day the music dies, the party's over.

ACKNOWLEDGMENTS

Thank you to anyone who has ever read anything I've written, going all the way back. Without you, there is no point. So thank you.

Thank you David Boies for simply being yourself. In an overrated world, you are underrated, because you are the most amazing person ever. So thank you for existing at all. You're the best.

Thank you Jack Balkin, Robert Post, Harold Koh, Megan Barnett and all at Yale Law School for so much more than a legal education.

Thank you Mink Choi and all at Thought Catalog for making this project at all possible. It takes a lot of great people to make a book. Mink, you are awesome. You have no idea. Truly.

Thank you Molly Oswaks for getting this whole thing started and so much more, etc et al.

Thank you David Samuels for the longest conversation ever. To be continued forever.

Thank you to everyone who was mentioned in this piece, living, dead and whatever else. You are giants.

Thank you Augusta (woof) for being the best thing ever.

Thank you Jim Freed for being the love of my life.

And thank you to everyone else, especially some people, you know who you are.

ABOUT THE
AUTHOR

ELIZABETH WURTZEL is the author of *Prozac Nation*, *Bitch*, and *More, Now, Again*. She was the pop music critic at *New York Magazine* and *The New Yorker*. Her writing has appeared in *The New York Times*, *The Atlantic*, *The Wall Street Journal*, *The Oxford American*, *The Guardian* and many other publications. A graduate of Harvard College and Yale Law School, she is a lawyer at Boies, Schiller & Flexner. Elizabeth Wurtzel lives in Greenwich Village.

ABOUT THOUGHT CATALOG BOOKS

In late 2012, Thought Catalog Books launched as an outlet to experiment with long-form writing and paid reading experiences. For numerous reasons, we wanted to give our own writers and creatives in the extended Thought Catalog community the ability to write in this self-contained environment, allowing them to explore a different, often more contemplative medium for their expression. This is still the driving impulse of Thought Catalog Books years later.

We're trying to cut out the fluff so that we can empower our writers with the right tools and help them actualize their publishing careers — whether that's in philosophy, personal narrative, science fiction, young adult, literary fiction, crime writing, etc.

Submit your manuscript today for review: manuscripts@thoughtcatalog.com.